Praise for *4000 Miles*

"Herzog unravels the det: skill
. . . Everything about *400*   ılau-
sible . . . The family dran   the
best play of the season."

—Richard Zoglin, *Time*

"Herzog's wonderful play about growing up and finding home has only ripened over time. *4000 Miles* is one of the best, bravest plays of the season. See it no matter how far you must travel."

—David Cote, *Time Out New York*

"Plays as truthful and touching and fine as Amy Herzog's *4000 Miles* come along once or maybe twice a season, if we're lucky . . . A beautifully rendered portrait of the relationship between an old-style lefty grandmother and her new-style lefty grandson . . . This is the rare theatrical production that achieves perfection on its own terms."

—Charles Isherwood, *New York Times*

"Amy Herzog is an intelligent, delicately articulate writer with a piquant, arresting subject . . . Encounters of the kind Herzog graphs, compassionately, among left-thinking people, end irresolutely, or dissipate into nothing, giving her play the unresolved, undramatic quality of a set of short stories. Like the landed gentry who populate Chekhov's plays, Herzog's people are conscious of a large absence in their lives, but not wholly able to define it . . . She has a naturalistic delicacy of detail."

—Michael Feingold, *Village Voice*

"The best new play by a young writer . . . Part of its excellence arises from the seemingly paradoxical fact that Ms. Herzog has had the good sense not to make *4000 Miles* a political drama . . . It is, instead, a finely wrought, closely observed character study, funny and serious in just the right proportions."

—Terry Teachout, *Wall Street Journal*

Praise for *After the Revolution*

"As its fiery title implies, *After the Revolution* has more on its mind than recycling familiar grievances for a couple hours of entertainment . . . A smart, engrossing play."

—Charles Isherwood, *New York Times*

"Amy Herzog's smart, finely written *After the Revolution* is a shrewd, ironic meditation on what we do with history, how we appropriate it for our own psychological needs. Among the play's many pleasures—a firm grasp of historical paradox, sharp dialogue—the most satisfying is the way the characters struggle through their differences to listen to one another. The ability to listen is, perhaps, the definition of love."

—John Lahr, *New Yorker*

"*After the Revolution* is a smart, funny and provocative play. Herzog deftly avoids simple-minded polemics in favor of richly detailed people who are as ready to examine their relationships as they are their consciences . . . Written with an extraordinary balance of insight, humor and surprise, it's totally engaging."

—Frank Rizzo, *Variety*

"The intelligent, warm *After the Revolution* is sharp, funny and emotionally wise. This cantankerous, political family is one you'll want to spend time with—indeed, it's one many New Yorkers will feel like they already have."

—Jesse Oxfeld, *New York Observer*

"Amy Herzog's *After the Revolution* sounds, from both its title and plot synopsis, like a political drama. But while politics are most definitely involved, at its heart it's a family story of generational conflict. And as delivered, it's a damn good one."

—Erik Haagensen, *Backstage*

4000 Miles

After the Revolution

Books by Amy Herzog
Published by TCG

4000 Miles and *After the Revolution*

Belleville (forthcoming)

The Great God Pan (forthcoming)

4000 Miles

After the Revolution

TWO PLAYS

Amy Herzog

THEATRE COMMUNICATIONS GROUP   NEW YORK   2013

4000 Miles and *After the Revolution* are published by Theatre Communications Group, Inc., 520 8th Avenue, 24th Floor, New York, NY 10018-4156

The publication of *4000 Miles* and *After the Revolution*, by Amy Herzog, through TCG's Book Program, is made possible in part by the New York State Council on the Arts with the support of Governor Andrew Cuomo and the New York State Legislature.

TCG books are exclusively distributed to the book trade by Consortium Book Sales and Distribution.

LIBRARY OF CONGRESS CATALOGING-IN-PUBLICATION DATA

Herzog, Amy.
[Plays. Selections]
4000 miles and After the revolution : two plays / Amy Herzog. —First edition.
pages cm
ISBN 978-1-55936-422-5 (trade paper)
1. Families—Drama. 2. Intergenerational relations—Drama.
3. Domestic drama, American. I. Herzog, Amy. 4000 miles. II. Herzog, Amy. After the revolution. III. Title. IV. Title: After the revolution.
PS3608.E79A6   2013
812'.6—dc23   2013002065

Book design and composition by Lisa Govan
Cover design by Carol Devine Carson
First Edition, May 2013
Second Printing, March 2021

Contents

After the Revolution

For J. J. J.

After the Revolution was commissioned by and received its world premiere at the Williamstown Theatre Festival (Nicholas Martin, Artistic Director; Joe Finnegan, General Manager) in Williamstown, Massachusetts, on July 21, 2010. The production was directed by Carolyn Cantor. The set design was by Clint Ramos, the costume design was by Kaye Voyce, the lighting design was by Ben Stanton, the sound design and original music were by Fitz Patton and the production stage manager was Hannah Cohen. The cast was:

BEN JOSEPH	Peter Friedman
MEL	Mare Winningham
LEO JOSEPH	Mark Blum
VERA	Lois Smith
EMMA JOSEPH	Katharine Powell
MIGUEL	Elliot Villar
MORTY	David Margulies
JESS	Meredith Holzman
WAITER	Will Crouse

This production of *After the Revolution* transferred to Playwrights Horizons (Tim Sanford, Artistic Director; Leslie Marcus, Managing Director; Carol Fishman, General Manager) in New York City on November 10, 2010.

Characters

BEN JOSEPH	Joe's middle child, forty-nine
MEL	Ben's partner, female, late forties
LEO JOSEPH	Joe's oldest, fifty-two
VERA	Joe's second wife, eighty-two
EMMA JOSEPH	Ben's younger daughter, an activist, twenty-six
MIGUEL	Emma's boyfriend, twenty-six
MORTY	A donor to Emma's fund, seventy-six
JESS	Ben's older daughter, twenty-eight

Time and Place

The play takes place in New York and Boston in May and June of 1999: a year and a half after Joe Joseph's death.

Note

A slash (/) indicates overlapping dialogue.

Act One

Scene 1

May 1999.
> *Vera's apartment on West 10th Street, early evening.*
> *The mood is ebullient, though everyone is tired.*

BEN: So it's this program, kids from the projects in Roxbury are bused out to our school, there's grant money in it for us and it allows our superintendent to pat herself on the back but she doesn't actually take / any responsibility for—

MEL: It's a scandal, it's / really—

BEN: So these kids get a bus ride, but they don't get help buying textbooks, or paper, they don't get computers— they're supposed to use our computer lab but then they'd miss their / bus home—

MEL: And then they're penalized / for—

BEN: And then it's a big surprise they aren't passing their classes. Our principal calls a meeting, all these kids and their parents, half the parents don't show, / big surprise—

LEO: Right.

MEL: They're working three jobs, they're gonna come out to the suburbs because their kid's not passing math? I mean this is / their biggest—

LEO: God.

BEN: So the principal is standing up there / *lecturing*—

MEL: This guy is—he should *not* be in education, he has this / punitive—

BEN: The sense is *we are giving your children this opportunity and they are / squandering it*—

MEL: Which is—

BEN: And you can see these parents, the ones who have missed their shift at—Rite Aid or—to be here, they're just glazing over, I mean, they're so / alienated—

MEL: So Ben stands up, / I wish I was there.

BEN: I had been kind of hiding in the—so I stand up and I say my name is Ben Joseph, and I teach history and social justice here, and I'm a Marxist, and I don't think the problem is your children, I think the problem is our society the product of which is this school. I'm sorry that we have failed you, and I want to work with you and your children for change.

MEL: I *wish* I had been there.

LEO: And the principal?

MEL: Forget / it.

BEN: Furious. Goes white. Tries to bring the conversation back to personal responsibility.

MEL: But in the meantime Ben has them working on a list of / —what was it?

BEN: I said this meeting shouldn't be about us telling you what *we* need, you should be doing the talking, what do you need?

LEO: Good for you, bro.

MEL: What Benji's not telling you is that he told these kids at the beginning of the year that if they wanted extra help after school and they missed their bus, he would *drive them home*, you know, forty-five minutes to—and a lot of them took him up on it.

(Brief pause.)

BEN: And what about you, how were your classes this semester?
LEO: My—I was on sabbatical, I didn't tell you that?
BEN: But you didn't travel? . . .
LEO: Nah, just stayed home to work on the book.
BEN: The same one?
MEL: Don't say it like that.
BEN: Like what? I said / it neutrally.
MEL: It takes a long time to write a book. It takes me a long time to *read* a book.
LEO: The answer is yes. Same one.

(Brief pause.)

Sammy's been having a big season, you know, with the baseball, so it's been good to be around for that, especially since Beth is working again.
BEN: Well. Standing offer. Trade for a day. Anytime you want to come to Brookline and teach six periods a day I'll swing over to Tufts and do one of your sociology lectures.

(Vera has entered. She is sprightly at eighty-two, but fragile, and maybe a little off balance.)

VERA: Has the graduate arrived?
MEL: Not yet.
VERA: What do you think is taking her so long?
LEO: Well the subways were a mess getting / downtown.
BEN: Nah, if I know my daughter, she's on the phone with a journalist, or a / senator—
MEL: She really can't stop working, I think it's a / problem.

9

BEN: It's not a problem for all the people she's helping, I'll tell you that.

VERA: Well will somebody come taste my eggplant?

LEO: Your eggplant is perfect, take a load off, join us.

VERA: Well—

MEL: Sit, Vera!

LEO: Here, take my chair.

VERA: I guess I'll allow that.

BEN: We were telling / Leo—

VERA: Louder.

BEN: I was telling my big bro about that meeting, with the parents / of the—

VERA: Oh, about the black kids. *(To Leo)* Isn't that outrageous, what passes for a, whaddayacallit. / A social program.

BEN: They're actually—they're about seventy percent African American, / thirty percent Latino.

VERA: What?

BEN: They're not all black!

(Brief pause.)

VERA: Who?

(Ben laughs and shakes his head.)

LEO *(To Vera)*: Doesn't he look more and more like Dad?

MEL *(To Leo)*: Oh God, I know, it's uncanny.

BEN: What?

MEL, LEO AND VERA: You look like Joe/Dad.

(Leo says "Dad" where Mel and Vera say "Joe.")

VERA: And you sound like him. And your politics are like his. And I think all in all it's pretty wonderful, but that's just what I think.

(Brief pause.)

BEN: I was wishing he could've seen Emma up there today.

VERA: Well, he couldn't, and that's that. But then again he also can't see how all the rest of the grandchildren aren't in the political scene at all. So maybe it's for the best.

LEO *(An attempt at light-heartedness)*: Not talking about *my* kids, are you, Vera?

VERA: Yes, I am, I'm talking about Jake, and Katie, and, uh . . .

LEO: Sammy.

VERA: Right, and all of Janie's kids. They're all very nice people and so on and so forth, but they're not political. It's not a criticism, it's just an observation.

LEO: You're my stepmother and I love you but I think it was / a criticism.

MEL: I've always hated that word, stepmother, I've heard in French what they say is beautiful mother, now isn't that nicer?

VERA: What?

BEN: She doesn't like the word stepmother.

MEL: It doesn't do you justice, Vera.

VERA: Oh. Well. You either.

(Emma enters.)

EMMA: Sorry I'm / late.

(Everyone stands, bursts into applause, cries of Hey! Brava! etc.)

Stop it. Stop stop stop. I love you all, now shut up.

BEN: Get over here, kid.

(She goes to her dad, who bear hugs her.)

EMMA: Was it okay?

BEN: Was it okay? Was it *okay*?

EMMA: I couldn't hear myself at all.

(She hugs Mel.)

MEL: God I'm proud of you. You know what? Proud is not the right word because that sounds like I did something. I am *glad* for you.

EMMA: Thanks, Mel.

VERA: Emma?

EMMA: I'm really sorry, I was on my way here two hours ago, but Mumia's lawyer called, there's a development in the case and—anyway, sorry.

MEL *(To Vera)*: Can you believe the way she just rattles off his first name like that? He's a / celebrity to me.

VERA: Who?

MEL: Mumia Abu-Jamal.

BEN: What's the development?

EMMA: And it should have been a five-minute conversation but it never is, with Leonard, hi Uncle Leo, thanks for making it.

LEO: I wouldn't miss it. G&T?

EMMA: No, I feel like I've been drinking for three days straight.

LEO: Why break your streak?

(Laughter.)

VERA: Emma?

MEL: Do you want to lie down? You know, you don't have to talk to us.

BEN *(Laughing)*: Yes she does.

VERA *(To Leo)*: Did she hear me?

MEL: She's obviously / exhausted! Who wouldn't be?

LEO: Emma!

(Leo points to Vera.)

EMMA: I don't need to lie down, I'm fine.
>Yes, Grandma.
VERA: You could speak a little slower, and restate your point at the end. From the standpoint of propaganda. It was also too long, especially considering the weather.
LEO: Other than that, it was perfect.

(They all laugh.)

MEL: It *was* perfect. You are a / born speaker.
BEN: All those privileged white kids, their jaws dropping, like, "Did she just call me lazy? At my law school graduation?" / Fantastic.
LEO: It was good stuff, Emma. Tough stuff.
VERA: Well excuse me, no one told me that honest criticism was not allowed.
EMMA: I appreciate your thoughts, Grandma.
VERA: It seems to me you're going to make a lot of speeches, over the course of your—so it's good to learn something, right?
>What you said about Joe, and the blacklist, and—it was wonderful. It was just wonderful and I wish he could've heard it.
EMMA: Thank you.
MEL: Oh! Maxine.
BEN: Right. Your mom called here. She says big hug, and no pressure to call but she'll be up late if you can. *(To Mel)* Thank you. *(With an envelope for Emma)* And this is from Jane.
MEL: From Jane and Peter.
BEN: From—from my sister and that guy she married, right.
EMMA *(To everyone)*: You guys really didn't think it was too aggressive? My speech?
BEN: No.

LEO: You walked a line.

EMMA: Is that a yes, Uncle Leo?

LEO *(Equivocally)*: Uh, no, it's not.

BEN: You can't fight for change and be a nice guy, you can't / have both.

MEL: It was bracing. That's the word I've been looking for.

EMMA *(With the contents of the envelope)*: Oh my God.

MEL: She just made the whole thing out to you, so you can give half to the fund and keep half, or whatever, whatever you want, but she insists you keep at least a little bit for yourself.

BEN: I told her, fat chance.

EMMA: This is so generous.

LEO: That's Janie for / you.

VERA: From Jane?

MEL: From Jane and / Peter.

VERA: Well, they make a lot of money.

MEL: Is anyone else starving?

LEO: I'm getting hungry, / yeah.

BEN: We're still waiting for one, right?

EMMA: Oh! No, we're not.

MEL: What? He's not coming?

EMMA: Sorry, we both had so many graduation parties, we decided to split them up.

MEL: Well that's a big big bummer.

VERA: What's / the problem?

LEO: The real question is, did his family get to meet you?

(Brief pause.)

EVERYONE BUT EMMA: Oh!, okay, etc.

EMMA: Okay, his family didn't cross-examine me about my opinions vis-à-vis Fidel, Palestine, / affirmative action—

BEN: How did you end up such a high-functioning, socially acceptable young woman, coming from / this family?

EMMA: I ask myself that every day, Dad, / literally.

MEL: If you're with him I'm sure he has great politics.

EMMA: Good politics in my generation is different from good politics in your / generation, Mel.

MEL: We understand that, we're not dinosaurs, we're not Stalin apologists.

VERA: What? What about Stalin?

EMMA: You'll get to meet him / eventually.

LEO: Maybe he wants to come to the family reunion in August.

(General chorus of oooohhhhhhs and laughter.)

EMMA: Don't count on it.

VERA: I can't hear a word any of you is saying. Or maybe that was the point.

(The phone rings. Vera considers getting up.)

MEL: I'll get it.

(Mel exits.)

EMMA *(Loudly)*: We're talking about my boyfriend, Grandma. I told you about him, he's going to be working with me this year, on the fund.

LEO: I didn't know that. Not worried about mixing work and play?

BEN: A lot of great political couples worked together.

EMMA: We're not a "great political couple," Dad, let's keep the vicarious delusions of grandeur to some kind of / minimum.

VERA: What's his name again?

EMMA: Miguel.

VERA: What? /

EMMA: Miguel.

BEN *(In his best Spanish accent)*: Miguel Roja, de Puerto Rico.

EMMA: *Dad.*

VERA: What was the last one's name?

(Brief pause.)

EMMA: Carlos.

(Vera raises her eyebrows slightly but declines to comment. Mel reenters.)

MEL: Leo, Beth for you. *(To everyone)* She's sorry to interrupt the celebration.

LEO *(On his way out)*: She okay?

(Mel shrugs and nods; he exits.)

BEN: Well, before we adjourn to the dining room. *(Picks up his glass)*

MEL: Honey, I support everything you're about to say and just want to remind you that we're all really hungry.

BEN: I'll keep it short.
    Emma.

(Brief pause.)

EMMA: Do not cry, Dad, no crying; you'll make me cry.

BEN: Arright arright. As your father, and therefore a totally impartial, / objective—

(Interjections of "uh-huh," "right," etc.)

Shit, Emma, it's 1999. In this decade we saw the Soviet Union collapse and my dad die. Clinton is a big business president, the poor are getting poorer, racial divides are deepening, we're dropping bombs in the Balkans, and people are complacent. We're about to see a new millennium and it's hard to imagine things getting much worse.

VERA: That's a fact.

BEN: But . . .

EMMA: No crying!

BEN: Okay! *But.* A handful of things make me feel hopeful, and top of the list, no question: you, standing up there today, speaking for Mumia, for Dad, and I know we disagree about this word, but I'd say for revolution. And so I want to raise a glass and say not congratulations but thank you.

MEL: Hear hear.

*("To Emma," "cheers," etc.
Leo reenters, shaken.)*

BEN: And I didn't cry! And let's eat!

LEO: Benny?

EMMA: Thanks, Dad.

BEN: No no, that's the point. Thank *you.*

LEO: Ben.

BEN: What? I'm hungry, come on!

(Leo follows him off.)

VERA: Well, not in my lifetime.

MEL: What not in your lifetime, Vera?

VERA: Everything. What we were fighting for. *(To Emma)* Maybe in yours.

Scene 2

The kitchen, a few hours later.
   Ben sits with his head in his hands. Leo stands.

LEO: The good news is, we have some advance notice. If I didn't
   have this friend at Yale Press, the book would have come
   out, she would have been blindsided.
BEN: Shit. Shit shit shit.
LEO: This gives us a couple of weeks.
BEN: I honestly never believed this would happen. Those fuck-
   ing bastards.
LEO: Agreed, but let's not dwell on that when we need to be
   making a plan.
BEN: Actually I would like to dwell on it for just a minute, it's
   Dad, it's Dad's name.
LEO: And Emma has been invoking Dad's name publicly for
   the last four years and there are gonna be some conse-
   quences, I'm not sure if you understand / the depth of—
BEN: I understand, it's gonna kill her, I understand very well.

(Mel enters, perturbed.)

MEL: Shit, her hearing's gotten so much worse. I needed a break. I wish I believed in God and thought there was some fucking good reason for us all to go deaf blind and incontinent eventually.

Where's Emma?

LEO: She said she needed some air, which I know from my kids is code for smoking a cigarette.

MEL AND BEN: Emma doesn't smoke.

(Brief pause.)

MEL: What's going on in here?

LEO: We're sort of in the middle of something.

MEL: Benji?

BEN: I'm okay. Can you give us a minute?

MEL: Yeah, and then I'd like you to tell me what's going on.

(She exits.)

LEO: You should tell Emma in person, while we're in New York.

BEN: *Obviously!*

LEO: Okay, why don't you tell me how I can be helpful to you right now.

BEN: You could show a little outrage! A little indignation!

LEO: Uh . . .

BEN: Or is that too much to ask?

(Pause.)

LEO: Up to you, okay? But if you want me to be there when you tell her, I will.

Scene 3

Emma's apartment, late that night. Emma and Miguel mid-conversation.

MIGUEL: Your mom didn't make it?

EMMA: Are you kidding? She has chronic migraines, and gas is expensive, and . . . it's Monday . . . so. Of course not. Mel asked for your address so that she can send you her monthly newsletter about responsible consumerism (sorry). And my dad wanted me to convey to you a greeting in Spanish but I refused. He says congratulations on graduating.

MIGUEL: His Spanish is probably better than mine.

EMMA: His Spanish is most definitely *not* better than—what is that? *(He has produced a wrapped item)* No!

MIGUEL: Just a little—

EMMA: We agreed!

MIGUEL: It didn't really cost anything.

EMMA: I didn't know *free* presents were allowed!

MIGUEL: Will you please open it?

EMMA: I feel very betrayed.

(She opens it. It's a framed picture. She is moved.)

MIGUEL: For our new office.

EMMA: Miguel.

MIGUEL: Because I didn't think the decor should be left up to you, no offense. And I thought he should be up there.

EMMA: Where did you get it?

MIGUEL: You can just write in to the *Times*, they have this archive, they'll send you a print of any—because it's what they ran when he testified.

EMMA: It's so weird to see him without his glasses, especially toward the end he had these thick, like magnifying glasses on his . . . he just looks so vulnerable.

MIGUEL: If you don't like it.

EMMA: No—

MIGUEL: Because I know, it memorializes like the worst day in his life, but I thought it would be good, to—you know, to honor that.

But I completely understand if you—

EMMA: I love it.

(She kisses him.)

I can't wait to tell my dad and Mel you did this.
(Off his look) What?

MIGUEL: Nothing, I just. I want to meet them.

EMMA: I know. I want you to meet them, too.

MIGUEL: So . . . ?

EMMA: So I'm just picturing my dad wearing his Che T-shirt and Mel saying over and over that you have an amazing *face*, and I know you'll rise above it but I'll be humiliated, that's all.

MIGUEL: What will I rise above?

EMMA: Seriously?

MIGUEL: Yeah.

EMMA: Um, the insidious brand of leftist racism in my family?

MIGUEL: You're saying they're going to be welcoming to me.

EMMA: That is understatement.

MIGUEL: And I should take that to be racist.

(Pause.)

EMMA: Do you think *I'm* being racist?

MIGUEL: I think you're throwing that word around.

EMMA: I'm just so surprised you haven't remarked on this kind of thing before.

MIGUEL: If every time a white person was nice to me, I thought it was racism? I'd lead a pretty dark life, Emma.

(Brief pause. Off her look of concern:)

Hey, stay with me.

EMMA: Sorry. I've just been fighting off the feeling all day that lunch with your parents was like an unmitigated disaster and you haven't said anything about it yet, so . . .

MIGUEL: What? No, no . . .

EMMA: Tell me the truth.

MIGUEL: The restaurant was loud, it was hard to hear each other.

EMMA: And they basically never said a word, so I was essentially yelling across the table for an hour and a half about—I don't even know what about.

MIGUEL: I told you they're shy at first.

EMMA: Yeah, but . . .

MIGUEL: What?

EMMA: You could've helped me out. I mean, you were like . . . silent . . . Sid over there.

MIGUEL: Silent / Sid?

EMMA: Why weren't you talking?

MIGUEL: I—I don't know, I just felt . . . kinda down—my parents were—I think they thought it was gonna be some kinda corny culmination of immigrant dreams, you know, Oldest Son Graduates from Top Law school, and it was cold, and boring, and their camera ran out of batteries, and . . . I told you they're not totally thrilled about me taking this job.

EMMA: No you didn't.

MIGUEL: I didn't? Oh. Well—it's not anything you should worry about, but from their perspective, it's like, I took out all these loans and now I'm making thirty thousand dollars a year working for my gringa girlfriend.

(Pause.)

EMMA: Ouch.

MIGUEL: But I don't want you to worry about it.

EMMA: Oh sure, absolutely, I'll just put it completely out of my mind.

MIGUEL: Emma.

EMMA: No, that makes me feel terrible, of course it does.

MIGUEL: Well it's not up to them. I'm doing what I believe in. Three years ago I didn't know what I believe in, now I do. If they can't be proud of that, that's their problem.

(Brief pause.)

EMMA: So I guess it wasn't the smoothest move on my part to monologue endlessly about the fund.

MIGUEL: Oh—also, with my dad's business, he's pretty tight with the local police, so the fact that our primary goal is to exonerate an accused cop killer . . . that's like the icing on the shit cake.

EMMA: Miguel!

MIGUEL: What?

EMMA: You have to tell me these things! I'm awesome with parents, that's like one of my primary characteristics, I can't believe you let me fuck that up.

MIGUEL: We'll go out to New Brunswick, spend the night, they'll get to know you and they'll love you.

EMMA: So it *was* a disaster.

MIGUEL: No! No.

Hey, at least you got to meet mine.

(Pause.)

EMMA: I'm going to see my dad tomorrow before he goes back to Boston, and I'd invite you, / but—

MIGUEL: Right, right.

EMMA: No, but he says he has something quote unquote important to tell me, it doesn't seem like an ideal moment.

MIGUEL: What do you think it is?

EMMA: I'm sure it's about Jess. I know this makes me a terrible sister, but I just don't have the energy anymore, if she's back in rehab I don't know why he can't tell me that on the phone. Do I sound callous?

MIGUEL: Yes.

EMMA: I'm just ready for her to stop torturing my dad; she's put him through so much.

Listen, be patient with me, it's just . . . if you didn't absolutely love him, that would be tough on me.

MIGUEL: I don't want you to think I haven't been listening but I'd really like to kiss you now, can I do that?

(She smiles. They kiss.)

Scene 4

The next day. Leo, Ben and Emma in the apartment on West 10th Street. Pause.

BEN: Uhhhhh.
LEO: Take your time.
EMMA: What's going on?
LEO: Give him a minute.
EMMA: Okay you're freaking me out.
LEO: It's okay. He just needs a little time.
EMMA: Well I have a meeting with a major donor / in half—
LEO: You're going to be late. Sit down.

    (She does.)

EMMA: . . . Dad?
    Is this about—are you okay?
BEN: I'm okay.
EMMA: Jess?

BEN: Your sister's fine. She's the same. Mel's fine—

EMMA: Then—?

LEO: He's getting there.

(Ben looks at Leo, who nods encouragingly.)

BEN: In your, uh. Research, or in class. Did you ever come across the word Venona?

EMMA: I don't know, rings a distant bell.

BEN: Soviet cables, between the U.S. and Russia during World War II. Some people got lazy, reused pages from the code book, it allowed American intelligence to decrypt some thousands of cables. This was known as the Venona project.

EMMA: Okay, yes, vaguely.

LEO: A few years ago a lot of this information was declassified. You may remember that the Rosenbergs—

BEN: Can we leave the Rosenbergs out of it?

LEO: I was just giving / her some context.

BEN: I don't like that context.

EMMA: I do remember, there was evidence of Julius Rosenberg's guilt, maybe, or maybe it was bullshit. I'm sorry, where is this going?

(Pause.)

BEN: There's a book coming out, it'll be in stores soon. It uses the Venona source material to name American spies for the Soviet Union in the forties.

EMMA: Okay . . .

And?

(Ben looks down.)

LEO: Dad was named. He has a two-page entry.

(Long pause.)

EMMA: Okay. Wow, that is—*wow*. So what's our strategy?

LEO: What do you mean?

EMMA: How do we fight it? We should issue a statement before it's reviewed. Have you been in touch with family members of other people who were named—or even better, are some of them still living?

LEO: Uh—

EMMA: We need to *move* on this, it's fifty years later and / they're still—

LEO: Emma, hold on.

BEN: She's right, it's exactly what I've / been—

LEO: She doesn't understand yet.

EMMA: What don't I understand?

(Leo looks at Ben who doesn't pick up the thread.)

LEO: We're not going to contest it. First of all, it's two pages in a five-hundred page book that almost no one is going to read. If it weren't for your work, for the likelihood someone will call your attention to it, we might not even be having this conversation.

EMMA: And second of all?

LEO: Benny.

EMMA: Dad?

(Pause.)

BEN: Look, I haven't read the copy, it could be total fucking James Bond fabricated BS.

LEO: Except that it's not.

BEN: You haven't read it either. You're just willing to accept / what some right wing—

LEO: Because we know it's true.

BEN: Not the particulars.

LEO: Not the particulars, no. But the essence of it.

BEN: I disagree; I think it's the essence they have one hundred / percent misconstrued.

LEO: Not having read it.

EMMA: One of you really has to tell me what's going on.

LEO: I'm going to get a glass of water.

(Leo exits.)

BEN: You know the history, I don't have to tell you that Russia was our ally in / World War II.

EMMA: *Dad.*

BEN: That Russian men and women were dying by the millions to fight fascism and we repaid them with stingy intelligence, by freezing them out of / the major—

EMMA: Stop stop stop.

BEN: Look, Leo would have it that we know something definitive about what happened during those years, but the truth is we weren't born yet and what Dad said to us about it was along the lines of, "We did what we had to do." I don't think that's as conclusive as my brother seems to.

(Brief pause.)

EMMA: You told me—you've always told me. That Grandpa Joe was blacklisted because he was an ideological communist. That's what I've been standing at podiums and repeating for the last four years.

BEN: And it's true, I firmly believe that is why he was blacklisted.

EMMA: But you're telling me something different now.

BEN: Well—

EMMA: Dad. When Grandpa said, "We did what we had to do." What did you think that meant, at the time?

BEN: Uh. In the context, which I don't remember that clearly. It seemed to mean that he passed information to Soviet agents during World War II.

(Pause.)

EMMA: Did you ever think about telling me?
BEN: Yes. Often.
EMMA: Why didn't you?

(Leo reenters. A pause.)

LEO: So this is gonna create some awkwardness for you.
EMMA: *Yeah*.
LEO: What you need to keep in mind: however ugly it gets these next few weeks, no one will remember in a year. You just have to ride it out. The work you do is still terrific. It's still true he was blacklisted, that's still persecution and it shouldn't have happened.
EMMA: No, he shouldn't have been blacklisted.
      He should have been tried for espionage.
BEN: Emma.
EMMA *(To Leo)*: Ride it out? The whole thing is predicated on his innocence; the fund is *named* after him.
LEO: That's maybe something you'll have to look at.
BEN: What?
EMMA: Mumia's detractors are going to have a fucking field day with / this, oh God, oh God—
BEN: You're telling her to rename the fund?
LEO: No, but it's something she may have to consider.
BEN: Emma, no, you do not bow down to these fuckers, you don't do that.
LEO: It's not about bowing down or not bowing down, it's what's politically expedient.
EMMA *(To Leo)*: I have to think about the consequences for Mumia, for all the people I've bound up in / Joe's reputation.
LEO: Okay, but take it one step at a / time.
BEN: You're a Marxist, Emma, you educate. You use your platform to explain what these bastards are doing, that it's

McCarthy rearing his head, that your grandfather dared to question the powerful and he's dead now and they're still not done punishing him.

EMMA (*All icy rage*): Dad. You sacrificed your chance to be part of this conversation when you lied to me for my whole life. Please stay out of it.

(*Pause. A stunned, hurt Ben returns her iciness.*)

BEN: Well maybe you can see why I didn't tell you, the way you're dealing with this. I guess I was right to wonder whether you'd do the right thing.

(*Pause. Emma gets her bag.*)

LEO: Let's not leave it like that.
EMMA: I have a meeting.
LEO: Let's finish the conversation.
EMMA: I have nothing more to say.

(*She exits.*)

Scene 5

Morty and Emma at a table at Gene's restaurant in the Village; Emma has just arrived. Two glasses of champagne are on the table.

MORTY: I'm very happy that we're meeting today because today is a special anniversary for me. Today I have lived in Greenwich Village for sixty years.

EMMA: . . . wow.

MORTY: I moved to Greenwich Village from the Bronx when I was seventeen years old and I never left. Even once I made enough money to leave, I didn't want to.

EMMA: Well happy anniversary. I'm so sorry to have kept you waiting, / I was—

MORTY: You're busy, I understand. I was busy once, too, I can faintly remember. How is your beautiful grandmother?

EMMA: She's well. I mean, she still misses Joe a lot, so . . .

MORTY: No disrespect to your grandfather, who I greatly admired, but as soon as she is fully recovered I hope she will go on a date with me.

(Emma laughs awkwardly.)

I saw her at the tennis courts in Central Park a few weeks ago, playing doubles. I told her she should call me if they were ever short a player, she said she didn't think she would. Just like that, she said, "I don't think I'll do that, Morty." I like a woman who's honest.

EMMA: Now I'd hate to think your generosity to the fund has anything to do with getting a date with my grandmother.

MORTY: Absolutely not; of course not.

Now if my generosity to your fund resulted in a date with your grandmother, I would not refuse on principle. But I have no expectations—none.

Now before I forget, last night I'm having dinner with some friends, and we're talking about which organizations we give money to, which is a way old lefties show off and pass the time and put off thoughts of death. I say, more and more I give to just one organization, the Joe Joseph fund. My friend, who is to say the least a financially comfortable individual, he says, I know of that fund, and I'm very impressed with the young lady who runs it, etcetera, but I've reviewed the facts, and that Mumia Abu-Jamal, I just don't think he's innocent. I said, well first of all you're wrong, second of all you've missed the point, the question is not simply did he shoot the cop or didn't he, it's did he receive a fair trial, was he set up, would he be on Death Row if he wasn't a Black Panther? I said have you forgotten the lessons of McCarthyism? We have to stand up when people are persecuted for their political affiliations. So how did I do?

EMMA: You did great, Morty, I'm afraid I've created a monster.

MORTY: Well my friend wasn't convinced. Here is his name and telephone number. He's a pain in the ass, good luck getting two words in, but you're more persuasive than I am, not to mention better looking, and if you can get him to come around he's good for ten thousand a year, easy.

EMMA: Thanks.

MORTY: I do what I can. I took the liberty of ordering champagne. Nothing too good for the proletariat, right?

(He lifts a glass.)

EMMA *(Gently scolding)*: Morty . . .

MORTY: Admittedly an extravagance at lunch, but you just graduated and I'll turn up my toes soon and everything I don't spend will be taxed to hell anyway.

To the most extraordinary young woman I know, who has given me something to live for in my decrepit old age.

(They drink.)

EMMA: You're not really that old, Morty.

MORTY: I'm six years younger than your grandmother; that's what you're thinking. But I don't think age should stand in the way of true love.

EMMA: I'm thinking that you have a lot of years ahead of you and you should act like it.

MORTY: Well that's a good segue to what I want to talk to you about.

EMMA: First / I should tell you—

MORTY: And I don't want any objections, I don't want a fuss, I thought about not telling you, but it was an excuse to have lunch with you and anyway you should know because it will help you plan for the future.

EMMA: You're scaring me, a little.

MORTY: It's very simple. I'm leaving everything to your fund. All of it; everything; the whole kit and kaboodle.

(Off her look) Now I said no fuss.

EMMA: But—

MORTY: That's all. My accountant will be in touch with you to give you an idea of the figures. You and I never need to talk about it again.

EMMA: I can't—

MORTY: Yes you can.

EMMA: Morty—

MORTY: Yes. You can.

EMMA: I have to tell you why this incredibly generous offer makes me feel so anxious / right now.

MORTY: Listen, I know. I knew you'd bring up my children, because I know how you feel about family. They're all right. They all make a good living at this point, with the exception of Kathy, who—well, never mind about Kathy. And I've given them plenty of help along the way. Now I'm not saying it will be easy to explain to them—

EMMA (*Forcefully*): But you have to, you have to explain it to them.

MORTY: I understand.

EMMA: You can't just let them find out after you're gone, Morty, you have to tell them.

(*She has gotten quite upset.*)

MORTY (*Gently*): Okay, okay, that's all right. I'm sorry I upset you. But I want you to listen to an old man on a soapbox for just a minute.

I was around when what happened to your grandfather . . . happened. I was what they called a fellow traveler, which meant I was never a member of the party but I was known to be sympathetic to those who were. Until things got really hairy, and then I kept my distance. From good friends who could have used my help, I kept my distance. Do you know, Emma, that to this day I thank God that I was never asked to appear and name names, because I'm almost sure I would have done it?

EMMA: You don't know that.

MORTY: It's my best guess. Men like your grandfather . . .

Who took the fifth, who took the consequences.

You are a young person with the courage of your con-
victions. It is my greatest and last honor to help you.

Now what was it you wanted to tell me?

Scene 6

Ben on Emma's answering machine.

BEN: Hi! Hey, sweetie. About our talk the other day . . . I'm sorry about how it went, and let's not have this silence, okay? It's eating me up and I think it's probably eating you up, too. I know you have some big decisions to make. I want to be part of that. I think I have a right to be a part of that. And I don't want you to do something you'll regret later.

I thought you'd appreciate this, though, last day of classes before finals today, one of my sophomores, I think I told you about him, one of my Roxbury kids, never spoke in class, one of those kids with the jeans below his ass and the big hood with the baby face under it. This afternoon he came up and thanked me for a good year. Told me he now considers himself a Marxist. *Not* what I imagined he was thinking all that time I was up front bloviating and he was carving shit into his desk.

So. I got one.

And I'm waiting for your call.

Scene 7

*Emma and Vera, in the apartment in New York, having just fin-
ished eating.*

VERA: So this new fella.
EMMA: Miguel.
VERA: Miguel. It's serious.
EMMA: We've been together since September.
VERA: Right. But is it serious?
EMMA: I . . . guess I don't know what people mean when they
    say that. I wouldn't still be with him if I didn't take him
    seriously.

(Vera chews, watching her.)

    What?
VERA: Didn't say anything.
EMMA: What, Grandma?

VERA: I think you should be honest with him, that's all. Because I don't think you're serious, and it sounds to me like he is. That's all.

(Pause. They eat.)

Have I told you about the lesbian who tried to seduce / me?
EMMA: Yes.
VERA: She showed up at the house, saying she had such a big, whaddayacallit.
EMMA: Clitoris.
VERA: Clitoris, right, and she said it would be terrific, and all that. And I said no thank you, and she went away. Nice woman. Very pretty, actually. But she had been, um. Whaddayacallit.
EMMA *(Reluctantly, but she knows every word of this story)*: Sexually / abused.
VERA: Sexually abused, right.

(Brief pause.)

Which most of them / have been.
EMMA: Oh Grandma, that's *not true.*
VERA: Well. I'm not saying all of them.
     But almost all of them.
EMMA: I could show you studies, it's not true.
VERA: All right, all right. I'm only saying, from my experience.
EMMA: This is all to say . . . ?
VERA: What?
EMMA: What's your point?
     You went from asking about Miguel to telling / your old lesbian classic.
VERA: Oh, because. You know your father hoped you would be a lesbian. You or your sister. Which I always thought was pretty strange.

EMMA: It's not that he / hoped one—

VERA: You have to talk louder if you want me to hear.

EMMA: It's not that he hoped we would be gay, it's that he wanted to create the space in—I still don't understand the connection.

VERA: I'm saying, just because your father wanted you to be gay, and you're not. Doesn't mean you have to go out with the kind of guys you always go out with.

(Pause.)

It's all right if you want to. It doesn't bother me. I just don't think you need to have a rule about it, to please your father.

EMMA: I don't have a rule about it. The last two *happened* to be Latino.

VERA: I think the fact that you're so sensitive about it, that's something you should look into.

(Pause.)

And I've never understood your prejudice against Jewish men.

EMMA: I do not have a prejudice / against Jewish men!

VERA: I mean you'll do what you want, you always have, but you should just think about what you could be missing in terms of a, whaddayacallit, a common, a love of, of, books, and thinking about the important things, and an easy way of talking to each other. That's all.

EMMA: Well, Miguel loves books, and he thinks about important things, and we have an easy way of talking to each other. And I hoped we could talk about Grandpa Joe.

(Brief pause.)

VERA: Sure. We can talk about Joe.

EMMA: I'm not sure how much my dad told you / about—

VERA: He told me about that filthy book, I know all about it. It's the first time in a year and a half I've been glad Joe is gone, so he never had to see that. Disgusting, Emma. It's just disgusting.

EMMA: I want to ask you about Joe's activities. In the forties.

VERA: We weren't married in the forties.

EMMA: I know that.

VERA: We were married in 1958.

EMMA: I know, Grandma, but he must have told you about that time, when he was working for the Office of Strategic Services.

VERA: That was during the war.

EMMA: Right. He was an economist in the Japanese Division.

VERA: Well, he was a brilliant man. Did you know he had just been appointed special assistant to Trygve Lie when they took his passport away in '49? That was when the UN was just really getting started, and he was a big part of it. He was supposed to have a brilliant political career, that's what was supposed to happen. Do you want dessert? I have some delicious plums.

EMMA: Thanks, I'm full.

VERA *(Exiting)*: They're very small.

(Vera exits. She returns a moment later with plums.)

What?

EMMA: What?

VERA: What did you say?

EMMA: I didn't say anything.

VERA *(Embarrassed and frustrated)*: You know, my hearing really isn't very good. I can't find words anymore, either. I say "whaddayacallit" all the time, I sound like a dummy.

EMMA: No you don't.

VERA: Don't get old, Emma.

Now isn't that delicious?

EMMA: It is.

Grandma, I didn't know until a few days ago that Grandpa was a spy.

(Vera stiffens.)

I'm hoping you can help me understand better what he did, and why he did it.

(Pause.)

VERA: Well. I'm not a rah-rah American. So.

(Brief pause.)

EMMA: What does that mean?

VERA: Just that I'm not a rah-rah American. If I were a rah-rah American I would see it one way, but I'm not, so I don't.

EMMA: I don't think you have to be a rah-rah American to question the ethics of spying.

VERA: That word again.

EMMA: He passed government secrets to Soviet agents, / what else should I call it?

VERA: Listen, Joe was a member of the Communist Party, you know that. Anybody with a beating heart and half a brain was back then, that's hard for people to understand nowa-days, because people have become so . . . whaddayacallit. Apathetic. But it's true. And the Russians were really the ones fighting the war, not us, and some people were very happy to sit back and let them die, even some people in the party, and some people like your grandfather were not. You're talking about ethics, well those were his ethics, not to turn his back on his comrades who were fighting fascism.

EMMA: So you're saying his allegiance wasn't to the self-interested U.S. government.

VERA: Right!

EMMA: It was to Stalin.

(Brief pause.)

VERA *(Flummoxed)*: Listen, you—he—a lot of what you hear about Stalin in this country is propaganda, it's / not—

EMMA: Oh, Grandma!

VERA: There were a lot of wonderful things about the Soviet Union! The papers would never report that because they didn't want the American people to know the / truth.

EMMA: Vera, / you can't do that, you can't pick and choose—

VERA: And whatever else you want to say the fact remains that it was really Stalin and the Russians who were stopping Hitler from killing all the Jews!

EMMA: Stalin was slaughtering Jews in his own country, and homosexuals, and / dissidents.

VERA: Well we didn't know that then!

And I still don't know how much of all that is true.

(Pause.)

EMMA: I should tell you that I'm thinking of making a public statement about this before the book comes out.

VERA: What?

EMMA *(Loudly)*: I may / make a—

VERA: I heard you.

What kind of public statement? The kind where you defend your grandfather against those bullies? That's what I hope you mean, Emma Joseph.

EMMA: It may not be as simple as that.

VERA: Well the question is which side are you on, that's the question.

(Brief pause.)

EMMA: Thank you for your time.

(She stands with some dishes.)

VERA: Leave those.
EMMA: I'll just put them / in the dishwasher.
VERA: I said *leave them*!

(Emma startles.)

Scene 8

Emma and Jess in Jess's small apartment.

JESS: And he's cool about working for you?

EMMA: What do you mean?

JESS: A lot of guys couldn't handle that.

EMMA: He's a feminist.

JESS: Yeah, he's dating you, it goes without saying he's a feminist, but . . .

EMMA: What?

JESS: No, if it's working, it's working. I mean, *I* would not want to be your employee, I give him a lot of credit.

EMMA: What about you? New man in your life?

JESS: No, my year's not quite up yet.

EMMA: Your—?

JESS: Oh. You're not supposed to date anyone until you've been out for at least a year.

EMMA: Oh. Oh.

JESS: No need to be embarrassed.

EMMA: I'm not.

JESS: You are, but it's cool.

(Brief pause.)

Mel said your speech was incredible.

EMMA: You talked to Mel?

JESS: We talk on Sundays. Sometimes Dad gets on the phone, if he's not feeling too emotionally fragile. Which he was this week.

EMMA: Are you serious? He won't get on the phone with you?

JESS: Not out of malice, he just—you know him, he gets upset.

EMMA: I just think that's incredibly fucked-up.

JESS: Whoa, negative words about our father?

EMMA: I'm shocked.

JESS: Well. It's not like you're calling me every Sunday, Sis.

EMMA: I'm sorry.

JESS: Yeah, let's not do that, I'm just making the point that it can be a challenge to have an addict in the family, I'm done throwing the blame around.

EMMA *(The sarcasm slips out)*: That's clear.

(Brief pause.)

JESS: What?

(Emma shakes her head.)

EMMA: So I actually need to tell you something.

JESS: Yeah, I thought it was a long trip just for a visit.

EMMA: This is going to be really hard. But I was very hurt that no one told me, and I made it a priority to come tell you in person.

JESS: Okay. I'm listening.

EMMA: Grandpa Joe spied for the Russians during World War II.

(Pause. No discernible reaction from Jess.)

JESS: I'm just thinking about how to respond to this.
EMMA: I know. I know.
JESS: No, um. I don't think you do. Actually.
 Sweetie, I already knew that.
 Should I not have told you that?
EMMA *(Forced calm)*: How did you know?
JESS: Dad told me.

(Brief pause.)

EMMA: When?
JESS: When? Um. Three? No four. Four? Years ago?
EMMA: Four *years* ago?
JESS: It was right after the first time I got out of rehab, so that was . . . '95. Yeah, about four years ago.
EMMA: How did it . . . / come up?
JESS: Funny story, actually. It was when he took me on that trip to London, that "you got out of rehab" reward, penitent-father-fucked-up-daughter-bonding-type-thing. And while we were there he took me to Marx's grave. Not first on my list of tourist attractions but also not up for debate. And he started crying. Which I found to be over the top. I asked him what was wrong, and that's when he told me.
EMMA: He said Grandpa was a spy.
JESS: That was the gist of it. And I was kind of like, I appreciate your sharing this huge thing with me, but we both know the real reason you're crying is that I'm such a colossal disappointment so let's not dress it up, you know?
EMMA: 1995 was the year I started the Joe Joseph fund.
JESS: Okay.
EMMA: It just seems like it might have come up.
JESS: I was back in rehab three weeks later, so it wasn't strictly speaking my tip-top priority.

EMMA: Well I guess that's the end of the conversation.

JESS: What does that mean?

EMMA: That's how you avoid every tough subject, that's how you recuse yourself from being part of our family, I'm not sure if you're aware of that.

JESS: He specifically asked me not to tell you. That's why I didn't say anything.

I'm sorry you put me in a position where I had to tell you that.

(Brief pause.)

You know in group I talk about you a lot. About how I feel bad that you didn't really get to have a childhood, fucked-up as I was.

EMMA: I'm sorry, but I'm not sure what the right response is to that. Is it thank you?

(Pause. Jess takes this with some grace.)

JESS: Are you staying with Dad and Mel, while you're up here?

EMMA: No. With Uncle Leo.

JESS: Can I give you one tiny piece of advice? Punishing Dad isn't as fun or satisfying as you think it's going to be.

EMMA: I'm not punishing him.

JESS: Okay.

EMMA: I'm trying to surround the situation.

JESS: Well go easy on him.

EMMA: Are you *serious*?

JESS: The irony is not lost on me. Just some hard-won wisdom, or whatever.

(Brief pause.)

You gonna be okay?

EMMA: Am *I* gonna be okay?
JESS: Um. Yeah.

(They look at each other.)

Scene 9

Emma at Leo's house in the middle of the night. She sits at a table, drinking tea, poring over a document.
    Leo enters in his pajamas.

LEO: Sammy get home?

    (She startles.)

    Sorry.
EMMA: Yeah, a while ago. He made curfew.
LEO: Good. Sober?
EMMA *(Lying)*: What? I think so.
LEO *(He's not buying it)*: Good cousin.

    (She averts his gaze.)

EMMA: Katie's so grown up.
LEO: She's somethin', huh?

EMMA: She—while you and Beth were cooking she asked what I was doing in Boston and I started to tell her—

LEO: Oh.

EMMA: But I realized you—so I didn't say anything.

LEO: Thanks.

EMMA: But you should tell her.

LEO: Keep meaning to. Somehow it . . .

EMMA: Yeah. You should really tell them, though, all three of them, so they don't find out from the book.

LEO: I don't think my three jock kids will be perusing the non-fiction section anytime / soon.

EMMA: But you should still tell them.

LEO: I know. I will.

EMMA: Thanks for, uh . . . it's been really nice to be here.

(A warm pause.)

LEO: You wanna try to get some sleep?

EMMA: Soon.

(He begins to exit. Emma reads from a document.)

"Senators, in all dignity, in all self-respect, in all loyalty to the Constitution and to this country, I could not participate in the purposes of this committee."

LEO: What's that?

EMMA: It's your dad.

(She holds out the testimony to him.)

His testimony before the subcommittee.

(He doesn't come toward her.)

LEO: Where did you get it?

EMMA: Federal repository on Madison Avenue. Any of us could have gotten it anytime. I just said Joe Joseph and they came back five minutes later with . . . but I couldn't bring myself to read it, the whole bus ride up here, I just . . .

(He takes it hesitantly.)

LEO: Oh, man.
    "In all dignity, in all self-respect . . ."
EMMA: He says some really wonderful things. Really brave.
LEO: God, I can hear his, his—
EMMA: Yeah, I know.
LEO: You remember / his—?
EMMA: A little. I remember being scared of him and thinking he was the smartest person in the world.

(She sees that he is immersed in the document.)

It's amazing, how they keep hounding him, they ask the same question about two hundred / different—
LEO *(Reading, imitating his father)*: "Gentleman, that is the same question, and I have already answered it."
EMMA: What was your answer?
LEO: "I decline to answer!"

(They laugh.)

That's terrible, your dad does a great / Joe Joseph.
EMMA: No, it's good, it's good. I don't remember that well, he was so sick by the time I was . . .
    I should stop you there. In a few pages it gets really disappointing.
LEO: Why?
EMMA: He perjures himself. He flat out denies committing espionage, multiple times, they don't even ask the direct question, he just volunteers . . .

(He flips forward a few pages, finds it.)

LEO: Hm.

EMMA: So.

LEO: Has Benny seen this?

EMMA: I don't know. It turns out there's a lot *Benny* never shared with me.

(Leo looks at the front page again.)

LEO: May 26th, 1953.

EMMA: So you were . . . five? Dad was three. Janie would've been . . . I guess your mom was pregnant?

LEO: Well that's true. But what I was thinking was. The Rosenbergs were executed three weeks later.

(This had not occurred to Emma. They are silent. He hands the testimony back to her.)

Make me a copy?

(She nods absentmindedly. He kisses the top of her head, then starts to exit. He stops.)

When I was in kindergarten we made kites. As a project, arts and crafts. The teacher said we had to bring in, I don't know, fifty cents each, to pay for our materials, the kite sticks. I said, no need for that, I'll provide all the kite sticks for everyone; you see, my dad owns a lumberyard.

EMMA: What?

LEO: We lived near a lumberyard, I don't know, I got confused, or I was . . . building my dad up, bragging, you know, kid stuff. So I went home and told him we needed to get all those kite sticks. And his face. Just.

   Fell.

He had been out of work for years. All those kite sticks, we didn't have any money.

EMMA: What did he do?

LEO: What could he do? He wasn't gonna hang me out to dry like that. He bought the kite sticks. My mom must have been furious. That must have been a fight. Shit, that must have been a big fight. I keep thinking about that.

Anyway, sleep well.

(Leo exits.)

Scene 10

Emma's apartment. Emma and Miguel, late at night.

EMMA: And I *hated* my Grandma Tessie, I didn't even go see her when she was dying, because the myth I grew up with was she left Joe at the height of the blacklist for some rich guy, I mean that wasn't a myth, it was true, but I realize now she must have *known* he spied, she must have thought he brought this on himself, and her, and *three young kids*, who *she* was supporting while he couldn't work, and she didn't see it as noble, she saw it as stupid, and irresponsible, and just think, as everything was starting to come out about what was happening under Stalin, and she must have thought—for this? We are destitute? My *children* are destitute? She was seven months pregnant and he was standing up there, *denying*—

(The phone rings.)

Don't answer that.

(They wait it out. It stops.)

VOICE-OVER: You've reached Emma Jos—

(Dial tone. Emma plunges on.)

EMMA: And the legend about Vera, how she met him when he was penniless and suicidally depressed because he had no job, no marriage, he had lost hope in the beautiful dream that was the revolution, and she accepted him; she was *proud* to be with a man who stood before the committee and took the Fifth. But now that I've read the testimony I know he didn't always take the Fifth; he also lied. And I think it's very likely that Vera knew that too. So their marriage, it was like this tiny fortress against, against, against what had emerged to be a terrible mistake. Which they never acknowledged.

MIGUEL: May I say something?

EMMA: *Yeah.*

MIGUEL: Joe worked for the OSS during the war, that's when he was passing information.

EMMA: Uh-huh.

MIGUEL: What did he do there? I mean, what was he privy to that mattered to the Soviets?

EMMA: Well by 1945 he was deputy chief of the Far Eastern division, and he also, apparently, befriended some people in the Soviet division so he was passing intelligence about both.

MIGUEL: And this was useful to the USSR how?

EMMA: I've read everything I can get my hands on and none of it is very specific, but I can imagine that he would have gleaned from his colleagues in the Soviet division some— I don't know, strategies, or—that the U.S. was keeping from the Soviet Union.

MIGUEL: But they were our allies.

55

EMMA: Yes, but you don't share everything you know, even with your allies.

MIGUEL: I'm just not hearing anything that sounds that significant.

EMMA: Well obviously the Soviets felt it was significant because they kept working with him.

MIGUEL: Was he paid?

EMMA: No! And that is not the point!

MIGUEL: Maybe I don't understand exactly what the point is.

EMMA: He stood up and testified—okay, you know the picture hanging over my desk in our office? That picture, where he looks so broken, but so—I thought—*noble*—on the day that picture was taken, he took an oath, and then he—

(She flips through the testimony.)

He said, listen to this, he said, "Gentlemen, may you know this too, that I have never committed espionage!"

MIGUEL: So you're upset that he perjured himself.

EMMA: I'm—of course I'm upset that he perjured himself, but I'm also upset that—and the point is not that *I'm* upset, it's a matter of principle, that we honored him, we believed that he upheld the Constitution by fighting for what he believed in, openly, lawfully, and he was persecuted for *that*. So if that basic premise is a lie then what is it exactly that we are doing here?

MIGUEL: Emma, there is an innocent man on death row fifty years after all this bullshit with your grandparents went / down—

EMMA: Bullshit?

MIGUEL: Yes, and you have made yourself a key figure in the fight to free this man, and you have not returned a single phone call to *anyone* in two weeks, including a man who is trying to leave us four million dollars. So I'm very interested in the psychodrama of your family, but I'm also wondering some things, like, do I still have a job?

EMMA: Four million / dollars?

MIGUEL: That's the figure Morty's accountant quoted me, yeah.

(Pause. Emma takes this in.)

I mean that's . . . that's a game changer.

EMMA: Holy shit, yeah.

MIGUEL: Listen, stop me if I'm like way over the line here, Em, but I think what's happening, with the book—it could actually be really good for you. And for us.

(She stares at him.)

I mean, I think it's about time you put some distance between yourself and your family.

EMMA: Okay.

MIGUEL: It's just, it's a different time now and I think maybe this will help you move forward in a really healthy way.

Making the connection between Mumia and the blacklist was so smart, I mean it got the Mortys of the world involved, and you having this personal story obviously . . . but maybe at this point, it's, I don't know. Time to let that go a little.

EMMA: I see.

(He registers that this is really not going well and back-pedals.)

MIGUEL: Don't get me wrong, I have a ton of respect for your grandfather and his whole / generation—

EMMA: Uh-huh.

MIGUEL: I mean I don't think we can even know what they were up against, what those times were / like.

EMMA: You've been an activist for about five minutes, Miguel, you actually really don't know anything.

(Pause.)

MIGUEL: Well that's not true. And I think making our work more about Mumia and less about 1953 is not the worst idea. But I just work here. So I guess I'll go to the office and wait until you make up your mind.

(He exits.)

Scene 11

Ben on Emma's answering machine.

BEN: My question is are you not picking up your phone for anyone or did you get caller ID just to avoid me? Or are you screening? Are you listening to me, right now?

Pick up the phone, Emma. This is your dad and you're hurting me a lot. Please pick up the phone.

(Pause.)

I was reelected president of the teachers' union this week. I know you think it's time I retired and let somebody young with new ideas step in, maybe a woman or somebody of color, but honey, nobody with any real vision came forward and there was a lot of pressure on me to run again so I caved and I did. This is the kind of thing I'd usually like to talk to you about, see if you think I did the right thing.

Emma? If you're there? Please?

(Emma seems like she might pick up. Then, angrily:)

Okay, since this fucking machine is the only way to talk to you, let me tell you a few things you might not have thought of. When he first got involved in the spying, we're barely out of the Depression, that meant *thirty percent* unemployment, it meant you don't walk past a garbage can without someone elbow deep in it. This is the landscape of my father's childhood and young adulthood. Now who are the people speaking up on behalf of the destitute? The American Communist Party. Who is talking about racial equality, twenty-five years before the Civil Rights Movement? Same answer. Who is calling attention to the fact that Russians are dying by the millions fighting fascism so that American hands can stay clean? Same answer, Emma. So who is my dad's allegiance to? Is it to J. Edgar Fucking Hoover? Is it to a president who fully intends to sell out the Soviets once Hitler is out of the way? No, it's to his party, it's to the honest working-class Russians who are dying so that he can be free. So that his kids, and their kids, that's *you*, could be free. You want to condemn him from where you're sitting, kiddo, from your Upper West Side / apartment, fine, but he's my father and I want nothing to do with it.

MEL *(Having come upon him)*: Ben!

(Gently) Benji, Benji, Benji.

(She takes the phone from him and hangs it up.)

Act Two

Scene 1

June 1999.

> *Emma's apartment. Emma is in PJs, smoking. Miguel enters, quietly. She doesn't hear him.*

MIGUEL: Hey.

> *(She turns.)*

EMMA: Hey.

MIGUEL: I've been trying to call you.

EMMA: You have?

MIGUEL: Yeah, I think your phone's off the hook.

EMMA: Oh.

MIGUEL *(Finding the phone indeed off the hook, and replacing it)*: "Oh."

> *(The phone immediately rings. Emma shakes her head. They wait it out. It stops ringing.)*

61

EMMA: It's good to see you.

MIGUEL: Yeah, you, too.

EMMA: I have been feeling so terrible about / what I said.

MIGUEL: I know.

EMMA: No, let me say this, because it was actually completely not representative—it's not how I feel. At all.

MIGUEL: I know that, Em.

EMMA: Because I have so much respect for your work, I'm sure I haven't said enough that I think you have a fucking incredible political mind, and the left is very lucky to have you.

MIGUEL: I've also been told I have an amazing face.

EMMA: Miguel, I'm being serious.

MIGUEL: I know you are.

EMMA: I'm trying to tell you that I admire you, *so much*, and you've taught me a lot.

MIGUEL *(Truly)*: Thank you.

EMMA: And I also think we've been really equal partners up to this point.

(Brief pause.)

MIGUEL *(Unconvincingly, but really trying not to start a fight)*: Yyyyeah.

EMMA: Oh.

MIGUEL: No, in a lot of ways, yeah.

EMMA: You don't feel that way.

MIGUEL: Well . . . I work for you. I mean, it's your fund and I work for you.

I didn't think that was a controversial statement.

EMMA: It may not be, but it still makes me feel like shit, to hear you say it like that.

MIGUEL: How would you say it?

EMMA: I say you work *with* me. When people ask, that's what I say.

MIGUEL: But that's a euphemism. Isn't it?

(Brief pause.)

It hasn't bothered me, for the most part, I mean I'm a modern guy, and it is your fund, I came in / late.

EMMA: It obviously bothers you.

MIGUEL: Now it bothers me, yeah, when I'm trying to get Mumia off death row and home to his son and you're sitting here in your pajamas pitying your—

Sorry. Sorry. I didn't come here to get into another fight.

(He hands her a document.)

We finished a draft of the petition. Leonard wants your notes.

I told him you have the flu. Nasty, stubborn, 1918-style flu. I told him you'd be back at work any day.

(She stares at the document.)

EMMA: Do you think he's innocent?

MIGUEL: Who?

EMMA: Mumia.

MIGUEL: . . . what?

EMMA: I've been wondering. I've been wondering about a lot of things.

MIGUEL *(Calmly)*: I think he didn't receive a fair trial. I think he was railroaded by a racist judge, jury, and prosecution. I think there's no way he'd be on death row if he weren't an outspoken political black man.

EMMA: Granted, but isn't it pretty likely he killed Daniel Faulkner?

I just keep thinking, even though we're right about so many things, we're right he was railroaded, we're right the death penalty is racist, we're right the government systematically punishes vocal progressives, but even being right about all those things, the end result could be that we free a man who's guilty of murder.

MIGUEL: He's not guilty.

EMMA: But if he is?

(The phone rings. Miguel impulsively picks up.)

MIGUEL: Hello?

EMMA: No-no-no!

(Lights up on Ben.)

BEN: Hello! Hi. Miguel. Oh good, hi. It's Ben, Emma's dad.

MIGUEL: Hi Ben.

(Emma shaking her head.)

BEN: Cómo estás?

MIGUEL: Good. Uh, good. How are you?

BEN: I've been better. As I'm sure you know. Is Emma there?

(Miguel looks pleadingly to Emma, who turns away.)

MIGUEL: She is here. I'm, uh. I'm not sure if she's gonna get on the phone. Sorry.

BEN: Not your fault.

(Pause.)

You guys getting to relax at all? Going to the beach, or . . .

MIGUEL: No. Well, yeah, a couple weeks ago we went to this thing, it's called Midsummer Night Swing.

BEN: Midsummer Night Swing?

MIGUEL: At Lincoln Center, it's uh. Swing dancing, you know, they hire a / band . . .

BEN: Emma does swing dancing?

MIGUEL: No, no she really doesn't. At all. I don't either, but I can fake it. She . . . it was pretty funny.

(Miguel is looking at Emma. She looks back at him.)

BEN: Yeah?

MIGUEL: Yeah.

BEN: Well I'm glad she has you.

(Pause.)

Has she made any decisions about the fund? If it's okay to ask.

MIGUEL: No. She hasn't.

BEN: She, uh. When we first spoke about it there was some talk about renaming it; I'm hoping that was just, you know, heat of the moment stuff.

(Brief pause.)

MIGUEL: No, I don't think so.

BEN: Because, the idea that all these years later, she has to apologize for her grandfather's radical politics—that's, I don't know at your age if you can understand this, that's just the scariest kind of history repeating itself.

MIGUEL: But she wouldn't be apologizing for Joe's radical politics. She'd be apologizing that he spied for Stalin.

(Emma's hand flies to her mouth. Ben reeling.)

BEN: Well thanks for pickin' up.

MIGUEL: I wish there was something I could do.

(Brief pause.)

BEN: Tell her, uh. Tell her I'm sorry about that last message. And I'm not gonna call again. Since I guess that's what she wants.

(Ben hangs up. Miguel hangs up.)

MIGUEL: He—
EMMA: Please don't tell me. I don't want to know.

(Leo enters Ben's space—Ben's head in his hands.)

LEO: Hey.

(Ben looks up.)

Sammy has that baseball game today, I wasn't sure if you still wanted to come. I was gonna call, but I thought my chances would be better if I just showed up.
BEN: Is he pitching?
LEO: He's gonna try. He's having trouble with that shoulder.
BEN: Oh no, still?
LEO: Yeah, Beth's having a fit, but last game of the year, I couldn't say no.
　　He loves it when you come, you know. The way you make a fool of yourself yelling his name in the stands. That's one thing I've never been any good at, cheering at sports games.
BEN *(Not a mean-spirited joke)*: Luckily that's the only thing.

(Leo throws something at him, if possible.)

LEO: Come on, it's a beautiful June day. What else you gonna do, sit here and stew?

BEN: Yeah, I had at least two hours more stewing on the agenda, followed by some brooding, and maybe a little moping if there's time.

LEO: I'll get you home by seven; you can do all those things then. It would mean a lot to him.

(The answer seems to be yes. Then—)

BEN: Emma stayed with you, while she was in Boston.

LEO: I'm sorry, she asked me not to tell you.

(Ben nods.)

Should I have said no? What would you have done?

BEN: I would've called you. Your kid? I would've called you.

LEO: I didn't know what good it would do; she's / an adult.

BEN: Still, I would have liked to know.

LEO: I can understand that.

(Brief pause.)

I told my own kids about the book, I sat the three of them down together, I might as well have said, you know, corn prices are falling in Kentucky. They were just . . .

No reaction. And I realized that's what I had been afraid of—not that they would be upset, but that they wouldn't. Because that's my fault, I guess I didn't instill, or. I failed to get something across about who Dad was, about who I am. Beth thought it was "interesting," that's it. She meant from a psychological standpoint. She always said Dad was needy, that he required a lot of praise, so it made sense to her, she said, that he would have done that. God I got so fucking defensive, I don't know why, her calling him needy, wiping out the whole historical—everything, with a little pop psychology, I just . . .

So anyway, Emma's been sort of the only person I can really talk to about it.

BEN: Lucky you.

LEO: I'm not saying that as a barb, just so you / understand.

BEN: You may not intend it as a barb but it feels like a barb.

LEO: I'd like to be able to talk to *you* about it, that's the point.

BEN: I don't see us ever agreeing.

LEO: There's a lot we agree about, you're focused on a very minor / part of the story.

BEN: We're talking about the difference between honoring Dad and shitting on him, that's what we're talking about.

LEO: I guess that's the main thing we disagree about; that those are the only two options.

(Pause.)

BEN: I appreciate your coming by. But I don't think I'm gonna come to the game.

LEO *(Sadly)*: Okay.

BEN: Tell him good luck. Uh, tell him watch that shoulder.

(Leo exits. Mel enters.)

MEL: Was that Leo?

BEN: He wanted me to go to Sammy's game.

MEL: Oh Benji, you should've gone.

BEN: Well. Add that to the list.

MEL: Please don't snap at me. I don't deserve that.

BEN: I'm getting a little tired of hearing from you about the things I should've done.

MEL: You asked me! You asked me what I thought, and I told you. Am I not allowed to have an opinion? I think you should've told her earlier, I do. But you didn't, so we're in this, and we deal with it, and notice I say we.

(Pause.)

BEN: Miguel picked up. Just now.

He said . . . he said he took Emma swing dancing. Can you picture that?

(Mel can't.)

MIGUEL: I think we should take a break.
EMMA: What?

What do you mean?

(Pause.)

Well I don't think so. I don't think we should.
MIGUEL: Uh . . .
EMMA: I think you're overreacting. I mean can we talk about this?
MIGUEL: We can talk about it, but I know that's what I want.
EMMA: Well I completely disagree.
MIGUEL: I'm sorry to hear that, but in this kind of situation, the person who wants to take a break wins. That's just how it works.
EMMA: What do you mean by "a break"?
MIGUEL: You could make this a little easier for me, Em.
EMMA: Are you breaking up with me?
MIGUEL: I don't know.
EMMA: What do you mean you don't know?
MIGUEL: You're letting me down, okay? You're not acting like I ever thought you would act. And I need to think about whether I want us to make it through this.

(Pause.)

EMMA: Well if it makes a difference I do want us to make it through this. I don't need to think about that because I know.

MIGUEL: It does make a difference. But I still need to think.

(He picks up the petition.)

Will you read this?
EMMA: Honestly? Probably not.

(Sadly, he takes the petition with him, and exits.)

Scene 2

Emma and Morty at Gene's restaurant. They have finished eating and the check is on the table.
    A long pause. Morty's face a mask of pained kindness.

MORTY: Well.

    (Pause.)

EMMA: This morning I received my first nasty email about it from a, um, right wing . . . someone with an advance copy. But it comes out on Friday, so. More people are going to notice.
MORTY: Yes. They will.

    (Pause.)

EMMA: I hardly think I need to say that you're released from any pledge you may have made to the fund.

MORTY: Oh, / Emma.

EMMA: The last time we sat here you asked me not to make a fuss. I'm asking you not to, now. Let's just forget that whole thing.

MORTY: Emma.

EMMA: And please apologize to your accountant for me; I'm sorry I wasted his time.

MORTY: Listen—

EMMA: That's all. That's all. Okay?

(Emma takes the check from the edge of the table and opens it.)

MORTY: What are you doing?

EMMA: I'm buying you lunch.

MORTY: I won't hear of that.

EMMA: It's the least I can do.

MORTY: Give that to me.

(Emma puts her credit card on the check.)

EMMA: It's done.

MORTY: Emma Joseph, you take that card back and you give that to me.

(Cowed, she does.)

I don't understand this attitude. I don't understand it at all.

Am I to believe that this . . . detail about your grandfather's biography. Leaves you totally uninterested in continuing your work?

EMMA: It's not a question of being interested, Morty, I just can't continue.

MORTY: So you're putting an end to the fund. Is that what you're telling me?

EMMA: I don't see another choice.

MORTY: I am simply amazed.

EMMA: And I'm surprised, too, to hear you refer to what I just told you as a "detail." Considering the—well, the faith you put in my grandfather's legacy. I would think this would be pretty devastating to you, too, actually.

MORTY: And when did you hear me say that your grandfather never spied for the Soviets? When did I say that?

(Brief pause.)

EMMA: You—?

MORTY: No, I didn't know.

But sure, I knew.

We're talking the 1940s? Take a walk in the East Village, throw a stone you hit a spy. I mean you didn't *say* that. You say that, you sound a lot like a certain senator from Wisconsin who you do not want to sound like. But . . .

(A gesture to say, "It was true.")

Mostly we're talking about nothing, we're talking about, I don't know, a good recipe for soap. You have a good recipe for soap, you mention it to somebody else in the party, next thing you know you're meeting a guy named Nikolai on a bench, handing over your soap recipe so some Russian kids can have a nice bath. This is the kind of thing that would later be called "spying" and for these people life would become hell. Now your grandfather was in government, so that's different. It did not help the left in the long run what he and his colleagues, what they did.

EMMA: No.

MORTY: No. So, that's a lesson. And we move on. Right?

(Brief pause.)

EMMA: The story I was raised with was that it was the government that lied, and cheated, and conspired.

MORTY: Still true.

EMMA: Still true, yes, but Joe met Soviet agents under highway overpasses and handed over unmarked envelopes; he had a *code name*; that was not what I heard on my father's knee.

MORTY: You're disappointed, I understand. You're disappointed in your family. It's terrible, I know, but Emma, this is not an uncommon predicament.

And you ask me, it's not a reason to let down Mumia, to let down all the people you have promised to help.

But I see your heart is no longer in it, and I will speak to my accountant and my lawyer later today, if that's what you want.

(Brief pause.)

EMMA: I'm trying really hard to figure out what the right thing to do is, Morty.

MORTY: It can be hard, can't it? Even for very bright, well-meaning people. In a tough situation, to know what's right?

Scene 3

Emma late at night. Her phone rings. It could be Miguel. She answers.

EMMA: Hello?
MEL: Hi honey.

> *(Brief pause.)*

EMMA: Mel?
MEL: Don't hang up, okay?

> *(Brief pause.)*

> Your dad's asleep, it's just me calling.
>   How are you?
EMMA: Fine.
MEL: Good. I'm fine, too. Your sister is doing really well, I don't
   know if you've talked to her recently, she's . . . I know bet-

ter than to feel sure of anything, but it's just incredible, how far she's come.

The dogs are fine.

EMMA: Good.

MEL: I just, I'm calling because I want to tell you about the time I did some civil disobedience, the *one* time, I don't think I've ever told you about it because it's a pretty painful memory / actually.

EMMA: Mel—

MEL: Honey just let me tell this story, okay?

It was the eighties, and it was for—never mind what it was for, who remembers, and I got put in jail, for, I don't know, a day, two days. You have to keep in mind, Emma, I'm a nice girl from the Midwest, this is *way*—being in jail, I'm terrified, I'm uncomfortable, I'm having panic attacks. Long story short your dad picks me up directly from jail once I'm released, we've been together maybe a year but it's before I moved in with you guys. And he takes me to Joe and Vera's. And I'm thinking, this is gonna be *great*, because whereas my own Republican parents don't understand what the fuck I'm doing with my life, Ben's parents get it. And they'll be *proud*. And this is my new *family*. You know?

EMMA: Uh-huh.

MEL: So we get there. We get there, and Emma, they never fucking mentioned it.

They went on and on about Leo, and especially Ben, and their political involvement and how they were so proud of their sons. And they didn't say one word to me about what I had done. What I had just been through.

EMMA: Why not?

MEL: Well when we left, I said, Benji, I was so hurt, I said, "Why didn't they say anything?" And he said, "The Communist Party didn't approve of the cause you went to jail for."

(Pause.)

You know it hurt your dad, too, the way they treated me, and I didn't blame him at the time. But looking back, I think why didn't *he* say anything? Why didn't he stand up to his dad and say he was proud of me?

Kiddo, I want to say to you that I'm proud of you. I know what you're doing right now is hard and I'm proud of you.

EMMA *(In tears)*: Thank you.

MEL: But I also have to say that what you're putting your dad through is cruel. Yell at him, curse, whatever, but you have to talk to him.

EMMA: I can't.

MEL: It's gonna be fuckin' hard. But yes you can.

(Pause. Big deliberate mood shift.)

Okay, end of speech, how's Miguel?

EMMA: Fine. No, not really fine, he's possibly very likely breaking up with me.

MEL: Why?

EMMA: I have no idea. I guess because I'm neglectful and self-righteous and can't admit when I'm wrong.

(Mel laughs.)

MEL: Well, you're a Joseph. You have some good qualities too.

(Brief pause.)

EMMA: Thanks for calling, Mel.

MEL: Love to you, kiddo. From both of us, *love to you.*

Scene 4

Jess and Emma in front of Ben and Mel's house. Emma stops short.

JESS: You need a minute?
EMMA: Yeah. You can go in.
JESS: It's cool, I'll wait with you.

> *(Jess takes out a cigarette. She offers one to Emma.)*

EMMA: No thanks.

> *(Jess puts the pack away. Emma goes into Jess's bag, takes out the pack, and takes a cigarette. Jess gives her the gift of not remarking on this. She lights Emma's cigarette.)*

JESS: Remember when I broke my leg sneaking out of that window?
EMMA: Do I remember? Oh my God, I felt so terrible.
JESS: That sucked.

EMMA: And you told Dad that I was asleep and didn't know you were sneaking out, and I never told him the truth, I still feel awful when I think about that. You were in that horrible contraption for what seemed like years.

JESS: Three breaks in one leg.

EMMA: Oh no.

(A wave of nausea.)

JESS: Are you okay?

EMMA: . . . yeah. Thought I was gonna throw up for a second there.

JESS: You're that nervous?

EMMA: Shut up. No.

(Pause.)

JESS: You know, this whole . . . thing. Has been really interesting for me. Because I'm suddenly like the good kid. I call every couple days, I come over for dinner, I'm like the silver-lining child for the first time in my life.

EMMA: You seem . . . really good.

JESS *(Quietly pleased)*: I'm um. Dating someone. Actually.

EMMA: That's great! For how long?

JESS: Well only about a week and a half, but it seems, um. Yeah.

EMMA: I want to hear all about him.

JESS: Uh-huh. Right. *Her.*

EMMA: . . . *what?*

JESS: Yeah. Yeah.

EMMA: Shit, you really are the silver-lining child. Is Dad thrilled beyond belief?

JESS *(Laughing with real joy and hilarity)*: Yes! Completely!

EMMA *(A little sadly)*: Wow.

JESS: Come on, it wouldn't kill you to be happy for me.

EMMA: I am happy for you. What's her name?

JESS: Leaf. She's a batik artist, and she's the most compassionate person I've ever known.

EMMA: That's, uh . . .

You deserve this.

JESS: Right??

(Pause.)

You ready? It won't be so bad; I'll be right there with you.

EMMA: It's funny: "Question Authority" was like a mantra we were raised with, but somehow that never extended to questioning *him*. For me, anyway.

JESS: For you.

(Jess stands. She pulls Emma to her feet.)

Scene 5

Ben and Mel's house in Brookline. Ben, Mel, Jess and Emma standing around awkwardly. A silence in which multiple people try to think of what to say.

MEL: . . . and the bus?
EMMA: Was fine. Jess was actually on time to pick me up, so that blew my mind.
JESS: I was *early*.

(They laugh.)

MEL: Are you hungry?
EMMA: No.
BEN: Jess?
JESS: Not yet.

(Another silence.)

MEL: So I'm just gonna come out and ask, do you two want to be alone? Or should we stay?

BEN: It's up to Emma.

EMMA: It doesn't matter.

JESS: It's up to you guys.

(Ben and Emma look at each other; no decision.)

MEL: Well can I say what I think? I think you should be alone.

JESS: I told Emma I'd be with her if she wants.

MEL: That's fine, too. Is that what you want, Emma?

EMMA: This is really weird and formal.

(Brief pause.)

MEL: Okay, I'm going to say again, though it's really not up to me, that my suggestion would be that you have this conversation alone.

BEN: That's okay with me.

JESS: Emma?

EMMA: Sure, whatever.

BEN: Not whatever, you should say what you want.

EMMA: Alone is fine. That's what I want.

MEL: Okay.

JESS *(Quietly, just to Emma)*: You sure?

(Emma nods.)

MEL *(Stagily)*: Excuse me, everyone, I need to do something upstairs. Jess, would you mind helping me do something upstairs?

(They make their way toward the exit.)

We are just upstairs. Should you need us.

(They exit. Silence.)

EMMA: You moved the picture of Fidel.
BEN: I figured no one got to see it in the bedroom, where it was.

(Pause. They speak simultaneously:)

EMMA: So we should—   BEN: How are you?

EMMA: What?
BEN: How are you? Just. How have you been?
EMMA: I'm okay. How are you?
BEN: Well . . .

(An attempt to smile through his misery is an answer to the question. A pause. Emma takes out a piece of paper.)

EMMA: I want to make sure I don't forget anything.

(Ben nods, perhaps sits, readies himself to listen. Emma refers to her list.)

I guess I didn't put these in a very sensible order.
BEN: That's okay. Whatever order you want is okay. I'm glad we're doing this.
EMMA: Um. The first thing I have written down is that I don't like the way you talk about the guys I date. I don't like it when you speak Spanish in relation to them, I don't like when you brag to your friends that I only date Latino men. I don't understand why that should be a point of pride to you.
BEN: Sweetheart, no matter *who* you date it's a point of pride to me, everything you do is a point of pride to me.
EMMA: I recognize the truth of that, on one hand, and you should recognize the truth of what I said.

BEN: I just—
EMMA: Dad, that's just the first one.

(He accepts this and listens.)

The second one. I'm skipping that one for now.

Oh. Number three is really small. It's that when I was little you made me call my Walkman a "Walkperson." I don't know why I . . . *(included that)*

Um. Number four

(Shakily) Is that you didn't tell me Grandpa Joe was a spy.

Number five is that you raised me to believe the revolution was coming and everything would be different even though you knew that was not true.

Number six is that it took you so long to realize Jess needed help. Because individual suffering has no place in Marxist philosophy.

Number seven is that you always rewarded me for my politics, and for working so hard, but never for just taking a break. And thinking. And being doubtful. And being sad.

Number eight is that I'm sorry.

Number nine. Um. I wrote again that you didn't tell me Grandpa Joe was a spy, I guess I forgot I had written that already.

And number ten *(Trouble reading it through tears)* Oh. Is that after Mel was in jail for civil disobedience in the eighties you didn't tell Joe you were proud of her.

(She puts down the piece of paper.)

BEN *(A deeply painful but real attempt to joke)*: That's *it*?
EMMA: I don't expect you to respond to all of it right away.
BEN: I'm going to respond. I'm going to respond to numbers four and nine first, since they were the same.

Uh.

I should've told you. I should've told you.

I have no excuse. I would like to explain the reasons, which are different from excuses, for why I didn't tell you, but only if you want to hear them.

EMMA: I don't know, Dad.

BEN: Up to you. No strings.

EMMA: Okay, what are the reasons?

(Ben takes out a piece of paper. The slightest acknowledgment between the two of them that this is funny.)

BEN: My dad didn't talk about it to us. He didn't even make an allusion to it until I was, I don't know, about your age. You can say that's because he felt he had done something wrong, that there was some shame there, and that may be true. But what's also true is that he was a man who lived in terror. Our phones were tapped, FBI agents hung out not far from our front door. The silence, that wasn't just a parental choice. That was a strategy for keeping him out of jail. And long after it was necessary, it was something that was trained into him. And I guess I picked that up.

EMMA: You told Jess. You told her almost four years ago.

BEN: That's true, and as I said these are not excuses. Not for nothing I didn't tell her on American soil.

EMMA: On—? Dad!

BEN: You can call it paranoid.

EMMA: I do, I do call it paranoid.

BEN: But that was part of my thinking. The second reason is that around the time I was planning to tell you, you started the Joe Joseph fund. You called and asked me to be on your board, you remember that? You said I was your "first ask." When you have kids maybe you'll know what that feels like, I *hope* you'll know what that feels like, to have a child grow up and say I've thought about it, and I believe what you believe, and I want you to be a part of it.

EMMA: You should have told me during that conversation.

BEN: But you had this powerful analysis about Mumia, and McCarthy, and the way this country still punishes the outspoken, that was so *smart*, I didn't want to. I don't know. Muddy the waters. Because what you were saying was right, the details of the history notwithstanding, it was still right, and people were paying attention.

EMMA: You're saying it was true despite the fact that it was partly a lie.

BEN: No, I'm saying—

EMMA: Dad, that's what you're saying. I need you to see that.

(Pause.)

BEN: And the last reason was, uh. A tremendous fear of letting you down. Which I have felt since you were three and a half, right after your mom left us, and I was a complete wreck. And you asked me very frankly one morning if I was too sad to take care of you and Jess.

EMMA: I don't remember that.

BEN: *Good.*

I heard your list. I heard it, and I'm trying to learn. Even at my age.

But I never made you call it a Walkperson; that / is fucking crap.

EMMA: You—?!! You did!

BEN: I did not.

EMMA: If I wanted one for the ecumenical winter holiday I had to call it a Walkperson, you must remember that.

BEN: Nope.

EMMA: Well.

You did.

(Pause.)

BEN: What was two? If I dare ask.

EMMA: Hm?

BEN: You skipped number two.

EMMA: Oh.

(She looks at the paper, though she doesn't have to.)

It wasn't important.

BEN: While we're getting it all out there we should be thorough.

EMMA: It's just . . . uh.

That I sometimes smoke. That's all.

And I'm twenty-six and I don't want to be sneaking around hiding it from you. So.

(A long pause. Ben has to squelch about a hundred impulses to lecture, berate, plead, etc. He settles on:)

BEN: Thanks for telling me.

Have you decided what you're going to do with the fund?

EMMA: I have.

BEN: Okay.

(He realizes she's not going to tell him.)

Okay.

Scene 6

Vera's apartment. Emma reads to Vera.

EMMA *(Reading)*: Dear Friends of The Joe Joseph Fund. Uh
. . . *(To Vera)* I'm gonna skip the introduction. Okay. You
okay?

VERA: So far you haven't said anything.

EMMA *(Reading)*: The first order of business is that it has come
to light that my grandfather, Joe Joseph, passed classified
government information to Soviet agents during World
War II. This fact came as a shock to—

    (To Vera) You know this part . . .

    (Continuing to read) I realize your support for the fund
may have been intimately connected to Joe's legacy, and
because of that I'd like to offer you the chance to have
your donations returned. An anonymous donor has
offered to make up for any lost funds, so your decision
to have your contributions returned will not negatively
impact our work.

That said, I urge you not only to let your past contributions stand, but to continue to make The Joe Joseph Fund a financial priority. We have reached a crucial juncture in the fight to free Mumia Abu-Jamal. This fall we expect the Supreme Court to hear our petition for—

(To Vera) And I go on about Mumia for a while . . . um . . .

(Reading) It turns out that my grandfather's legacy / included—

VERA: Louder.

EMMA *(Loudly)*: It turns out that my grandfather's legacy included activities that I consider to be dishonest and dishonorable. But it is his greater legacy, his belief in a society where regardless of your race or political persuasion you may speak out without fear, that I hope you will continue to uphold with your contributions and your support.

The other piece of news is that I am resigning as executive director of the fund. You can direct any questions to Miguel Roja, our interim leader whose wisdom and passion will guide us through this period of transition. I will retain my position on the board, and I will never be far from this organization in my heart and mind.

(To Vera) That's it.

(Pause.)

VERA: Well I think I know who the anonymous donor is. And I hope he's not expecting a date out of this.

(Emma laughs.)

I don't agree with a lot of it, but you know that.

I don't agree with your decision to leave it in someone else's hands. It's a family thing, or that's what I thought. And I don't know what you're going to do with yourself, besides.

EMMA: I don't know either, Grandma.

VERA: And I don't agree with what you said about, uh. Dishonorable. I don't agree with that at all, and I wish you'd change it before you send it out.

EMMA: I've already sent it out.

VERA: Oh. Then you're not asking for my advice.

EMMA: No.

VERA: Then I'm not sure why you read it to me.

EMMA: I wanted to share it with you. The conclusions I've reached.

VERA: Well. The fact is you weren't there back then so you can't ever really know what it was like. You can look back and say we did this wrong, or we did that wrong, but the point is it was *for* something. I look at most people your age, at your cousins, and I don't know what they're for. I don't know how they're going to feel when they get to be my age. When they look back and see how they spent their time. I look back and I feel proud.

EMMA: I feel proud, too. Of you and Joe, and my dad, I feel very proud.

VERA: Then why don't you say that in the letter?

EMMA: Grandma, I think I do. It makes me sad that you couldn't hear that in it.

VERA: Well. Every relationship has some sadness in it, right? That's life.

(Brief pause. She continues, not unkindly, but with incredible lucidity. Emma listens.)

Listen, what you've done here, my darling, is you've named your grandfather's name.

That's what it amounts to.

And—don't argue—you have your reasons, I understand that, I understand how from your point of view it's about honesty. But I met him after they named his name the first time, and it was a horror, an absolute horror. He spent the rest of his life recovering from that, but he raised his children to be proud. And not to be afraid. And to keep fighting. I spoke to your father, he told me he's forgiven you. He said it's healthy for you to be critical of your grandfather . . . he called that "progress." That's what he said. Well. I've lived too long to call it progress, Emma. And I love you and I'm sorry I can't agree with you.

But progress?

I'm afraid not.

No.

(Blackout.)

END OF PLAY

4000 Miles

For Leepee and Pavel, in memory of Jay

PRODUCTION HISTORY

4000 Miles was written for the SoHo Rep Writer/Director Lab in New York City. The play received its world premiere by Lincoln Center Theater (LCT3; André Bishop, Artistic Director; Bernard Gersten, Executive Producer; Paige Evans, Artistic Director of LCT3) in New York City, on June 20, 2011. The production was directed by Daniel Aukin. The set design was by Lauren Helpern, the costume design was by Kaye Voyce, the lighting design was by Japhy Weideman and the sound design was by Ryan Rumery. The production stage manager was Kasey Ostopchuck. The cast was:

LEO JOSEPH-CONNELL	Gabriel Ebert
VERA JOSEPH	Mary Louise Wilson
AMANDA	Greta Lee
BEC	Zoë Winters

This production of *4000 Miles* transferred to the Mitzi E. Newhouse Theater, Lincoln Center Theater (André Bishop, Artistic Director; Bernard Gersten, Executive Producer) and reopened on April 2, 2012.

Scene 1

The middle of the night.

    Leo, twenty-one, lanky, fit and dirty, stands just inside the apartment, his laden bike next to him. He is smiling broadly.

    Vera, ninety-one, tiny and frail but not without fortitude, is in her nightgown. Her eyes have not adjusted to the light. She covers her mouth because she hasn't put her teeth in. Her speech is altered for the same reason. She is quite disoriented.

    A pause in which he grins and she is uncomprehending.

LEO: You haven't changed the name. On the buzzer.

VERA: What?

LEO: The buzzer! It still says Joe Joseph!

VERA: So?

LEO: So you should change it. Put your name on there.

VERA: That is my name.

LEO: Your name isn't *Joe* Joseph.

VERA: . . . well . . .

LEO: Just seems like it's time.

(Pause.)

I can help you with that, if you want. I'm pretty handy.

VERA *(Slurred)*: You need a place to stay, is that it?

LEO: Sorry, what?

VERA *(Still covering her mouth, still slurred)*: You need a place to stay?

LEO: I can't understand you when you—

(He reaches to move her hand away from her mouth; startled, she draws back, almost losing her balance.)

Sorry.

VERA: Will you—wait here.

(She exits, still covering her mouth. He leans the bike against a bookcase and takes off one of the panniers—this takes some effort—it is extremely heavy. He puts it down on the floor noisily. Vera reenters, less disoriented, with teeth, and putting her hearing aid in.)

Are you high?

LEO: What? No.

VERA: Well it's three o'clock in the morning so I'm just asking. Have you eaten anything in a while?

LEO: I'm cool.

VERA: That's not what I asked you. You've lost weight.

LEO: It's been a long road, but a good one.

VERA: You biked all the way here?

LEO: Pretty much.

VERA: From Minnesota?

LEO: Actually we started in Seattle.

(Brief pause.)

VERA: There are some mountains in the middle, aren't there, whichever way you go?

LEO: There are. There are.

VERA: I'll get you a banana.

LEO: A—no! Whoa, jet fuel.

VERA: What?

LEO: NO SUCH THING AS A LOCAL BANANA!

VERA: You don't have to yell, it's only when you speak very low or very fast that I can't hear you.

LEO: I'm just concerned about you, I was leaning on that buzzer for quite a while.

VERA: Yes, well, I was asleep, and I didn't have my, whaddaya-callit, hearing aid in, and I wasn't expecting you.

LEO: Would you hear a fire alarm?

VERA: What?

LEO: WOULD YOU HEAR / A—

VERA: I heard you, listen, it's—it's the way you're acting I don't understand, actually, not your . . . the whole family's been very worried, I guess you know that. Your mother and father—

LEO: I'm sorry people worried, I am, but that's not something I can take responsibility for?

VERA: You should have called. You should have called your mother. She's been . . . she's really been . . .

(He picks up his pannier, goes to reattach it.)

LEO *(Warmly, apparently sincerely)*: Grandma Vera. It was awesome to see you.

VERA: What? —You're—

LEO: It's cool, I don't think either of us has to feel bad about the fact that the timing isn't right for me to be here.

VERA: You're going to—where will you go?

LEO: I have a tent and a camping stove and a love for the outdoors, I'll be all right.

VERA: You're in Manhattan!

LEO: Maybe you can give me a tip, somewhere out of the way?

VERA: There's no place like that! Listen, you're being—put that back down. Put it down.

(He hesitates.)

You can leave tomorrow, I won't stop you. Just—sleep here for a few hours, and take a shower, and eat some breakfast. I can wash those—you smell terrible and I wouldn't be surprised if you had lice.

LEO: I don't have lice.

VERA: And you don't seem all right to me, you don't . . . seem all right.

LEO *(Still smiling)*: It's just, if this is gonna be about calling Jane, and a last minute hellaciously overpriced plane flight for which she has to take a Valium because she's a phobic freak, and I wake up in the morning and she's here with a Valium hangover—

VERA: I'm not a reporter.

LEO: Meaning?

VERA: Meaning I'm not a news reporter and I won't call your mother if that's what you're asking me.

But the way you're talking about her, it's really not fair, a lot of people don't like flying.

LEO: Jane and I are at a juncture where more talking is not better than less talking. If that's not something you can understand, I'm saying it's probably best I go set up camp somewhere else.

VERA: I don't agree with it, but I understand.

(Pause.)

I know what she feels like is . . . if you're not talking to her, she just hopes you're talking to / someone.

LEO: Oh, that is bullshit, and you know her, and you know that is passive-aggressive *bullshit*! *She* wants to talk about it! *She!* I am fine!

VERA *(With genuine feeling)*: Well. I did want to say how sorry I am. That must have been—

LEO: Thank you.

(Silence. This has gotten to him, and she sees it.)

VERA: You what, came over the GW?

LEO: The—?

VERA: The George Washington Bridge?

LEO: I guess, yeah.

VERA: Was it pretty? At night?

LEO: . . . yeah, actually. Yeah. I'm not much of a city guy, but. It was all right.

VERA: I'm—I must say I'm surprised, and this is not a complaint, that you came here, instead of your—I've lost track whether she's your girlfriend or not, the chubby one, isn't she up at / whaddayacallit—

LEO: She's not chubby.

VERA: She's—well she's not *thin*.

LEO: She's healthy, she's / strong.

VERA: I don't see what that has to do with it.

LEO: She's not *chubby*.

VERA: All *right*. I thought if you ended up in New York you might have gone there.

LEO: I stopped by.

(Brief pause.)

VERA: She had another fella with her, is that / it?

LEO: No, Vera, she didn't have—it's just not good timing. It turns out. Which I respect. She said she needed to do some *thinking*. Thinking is good.

VERA: Well it's been a lousy coupla months for you then, between one thing and another.

(Pause.)

Would you take a shower before you get in bed?
    Leo?
LEO: What? Yeah. Shower sounds great.
VERA: You all right?
LEO: Yeah! Yeah.

(He picks up the pack and begins to head offstage. She stops him.)

VERA: Where are you going?
LEO: Guest room.
VERA: No, that one's my room now.
LEO: I thought that—I thought that was yours.
VERA: Not since Joe was sick. We moved in there for the, whaddayacallit, single beds and I stayed. Has it been that long since you've been here?
LEO: I was here for the funeral. I guess I forgot.
VERA: That was a long time ago. *(He hesitates)* You need anything else?
LEO: No, I—
    Grandma—
VERA: Yes?

(His uncertainty dissolves into a big smile.)

LEO: . . . good night.

(He exits.)

Scene 2

The next day, late morning.

    Vera enters through the front door with a laundry cart. She has some trouble maneuvering it through the door and into the apartment. She is taking care to be quiet. Once she has gotten the cart in and closed the door, she goes offstage to Leo's bedroom. A pause. She comes back, satisfied that he is still asleep.

    She takes the laundry from the cart, piece by piece, and folds it. Bike jerseys and shorts. Those wicking pieces of athletic clothing. Tiny cycling socks. She regards them all with some suspicion.

    The phone rings. At the first ring, she tenses, listens to see if she heard right. At the second ring, she looks anxiously toward the bedroom where Leo is sleeping and moves as quickly as she can to the old rotary phone.

VERA: Hello.
    Hold on.

    (She takes her whining hearing aid out.)

Hello.

(Mild irritation verging on imperiousness:)

Yes, darling, what?
 I'm not done with it.
 I'm not done with it yet.
 I know what time it is, but as a matter of fact my grand-
son is here so I've been busy.
 Yes, well, it was a surprise, he came and surprised me, so.
 Well that's—listen—
 Hello?

(She looks at the phone.)

Hello?

(She shakes her head and hangs up.)

Pain in the ass.

*(She goes back to the laundry and continues to fold, still peri-
odically shaking her head. After a few moments, Leo enters,
disheveled but clean.)*

LEO: Hey.

(She continues to fold.)

Vera.

*(She looks up with the startled look of half-deaf people who
aren't sure whether they heard something, and want to cover if
they did, and sees Leo.)*

VERA: Oh!

(She fumbles in her pockets for her hearing aid and puts it back in.)

The phone woke you?

LEO: No.

VERA: It was Ginny across the hall. I give her the arts section when I'm done with it and I'm late today. Never mind she's never given me a nickel for it, that's what I get for being nice. She says she's just checking in to see if I'm all right but you know she's really sitting there, stewing, resenting me, she's . . . well, no good deed goes unpunished, right? Did you sleep all right?

LEO: Mm-hm.

VERA: And then she just hung up! I told her you were here and she said, "Oh I'm terribly sorry," in this—like she was interrupting a big meeting or something and she just hung up without even saying—why it gets to me so much I don't know. She's just . . . *(She looks for the word, doesn't find it)*

She's really a character.

LEO: Huh.

VERA: But we have an arrangement where she calls me one night and I call her the next, and that way if one of us turns up our toes it won't take until we start smelling to figure it out. Which isn't really a problem for me, because I have the family, but she doesn't have anyone, so I guess I have guilt feelings about that is what it is. And we have a lot in common in terms of the political—we both, in terms of Cuba, and the pro-peace whaddayacallit, and being progressives, we see eye to eye, but in everything else she just drives me nuts.

LEO: You're giving her too much power.

VERA: What?

LEO: That power. You gotta take it back.

(She considers this.)

VERA: Well.

>If you stay longer, and I'm not saying you will, I'll show you how to, whaddayacallit.

>Disconnect the phone in that room, because I do get a lot of calls sometimes.

>You look better. *(Off his look)* What?

LEO: Good morning, Vera.

VERA: Actually it's after twe—

(He interrupts her with a big bear hug. Surprised, she gives in to the totally unexpected physical affection. The embrace goes on for a little while. She closes her eyes and tries to remember it. They separate. She smiles widely at him.)

>You smell better, too. What did you think of that bed?

LEO: It was great, great bed.

VERA: That's what I think! You know your Uncle Ben and Mel, they want me to get a new mattress. Which they do not offer to pay for. Every time they stay here they complain, and complain.

LEO: I slept like a rock.

VERA: I may quote you on that. I'll end up doing it, though, anyway, or else they'll have an excuse not to visit. You drink coffee?

LEO: Yeah, I'd love some.

(She exits. He surveys the neat little piles she's made of his stuff. He stoops and picks up a box of condoms that's seen wear and tear in his bag. He had forgotten he brought it. She reenters with coffee and a plate with a few breakfast pastries on it, maybe a couple hard-boiled eggs.)

VERA: I was glad to see you carry those and surprised they weren't opened. I thought you probably take it black.

LEO: I do.

VERA: Me, too, that's how I like it. *(He bites into a pastry)* Tell me if that's completely thawed. *(He gives her the thumbs-up)* I got a few of those free a month or two ago at the senior center, some event, they had a buffet table and at the end they were going to throw it all away, which I did not approve of. It was lucky I thought to freeze them because otherwise I would have had to go out and get you something and I wasn't feeling completely up to it. Some days I'm myself, and some days my head really isn't right, and my balance. It's really disgusting.

LEO: Have you had it checked out?

VERA: What? Oh sure, they're all useless, they just tell me I'm old and I knew that already.

I knew you were sleeping well because you didn't wake up when I brought your whaddayacallit out of your room. Moaning and groaning—that thing must weigh a hundred pounds!

LEO: Nah. About twenty.

VERA: Is that all?

LEO: Well that's one of four bags. Total weight's about fifty.

VERA: Fifty *pounds*?

LEO: More when I have food and water.

VERA: And you keep all that on your *bicycle*?

LEO: Yup.

(She can't quite believe this but has no alternative.)

VERA: Doesn't that make it a lot harder?

(He laughs, for the first time.)

LEO: Yeah, yup, that's a yes.

VERA: And you camped at night, is that it?

LEO: Usually. Sometimes I'd meet someone and be invited to crash.

VERA: You ever meet anyone really peculiar?

LEO: What do you mean?

VERA: I don't know, like some crackpot who wanted something weird from you, in exchange for . . . a place to stay or whatever.

LEO: Like . . . ?

VERA: Like a—whaddayacallit, something sexual, or—

LEO: *What?*

VERA: I would think on the road like that, by yourself, you'd meet all kinds of people.

LEO: I did meet all kinds of people. None of them required sexual favors from me, no.

VERA: If you were a woman it would probably have been different; you probably would have run into all kinds of things like that.

LEO: I know a lot of women who travel alone, Bec has done a lot of traveling / alone—

VERA: Rebecca—well, all right, if you're built like *that*, but I mean a smaller / woman.

LEO: I find if you approach people with love and trust you can count on getting the same things back from them.

(Brief pause.)

VERA: What is that, Confucius, or . . . ?

LEO: It's Leo Joseph-Connell. It's me.

VERA: I'm teasing you.

LEO: Okay.

VERA: I guess it's a sensitive subject.

LEO: Nope.

VERA: Well.

(Pause.)

LEO: You know anything about a climbing wall?

VERA: A what?

LEO: A climbing gym!

VERA: What's a climbing gym?

LEO: It's a—a gym. Where you climb. They have these walls / with—

VERA: Oh, with the funny, and you're in one of those whaddayacallit—

LEO: Harnesses.

VERA: Right, I've seen that. Where have I seen that? I saw that and I thought what the hell is that for?

(She gets the yellow pages.)

You want to go today, is that it?

LEO: I was thinking about it. Get the old upper body back to work.

(Now with the yellow pages, she asks this studiously casually, without looking at him.)

VERA: So you think you might stay a little longer, is that it? Would it be under . . . what would it be under?

(He takes the yellow pages from her, gently, and looks.)

LEO: Yellow pages. Man.

VERA: What?

LEO: Do you have a computer?

VERA: No, I—well yes, I have one, Ben and Mel got it for me, but I'm not, whaddayacallit. They were very happy with themselves for getting it for me but they didn't really show me what to do with it.

LEO: Mac or PC?

VERA: What?

LEO: We'll look at it later.

VERA: You know a lot about computers?

LEO: I don't like them. But I can use them.

VERA: I thought everyone your age liked them.

LEO: Micah never sent an email. His whole life. Which was stubborn as shit, but you have to admire it.

VERA: Did he use the telephone?

LEO: Yeah, but he didn't have a cell phone. I don't have one either.

VERA: I know you don't, I've been hearing about that a lot lately.

(Brief pause.)

I guess what they say is all this, whatsit, technology is good for . . . from the standpoint of the people, or the—that you can get the propaganda to the people, the Marxist—I can't find the words, but in terms of Africa, and South America, and places where—that from the standpoint of being progressive and so on and so forth it can be a good thing.

(Brief pause.)

You know, there are a lot of bad things about getting old, but the worst one is not being able to find my words. I just hate not being able to find my words, I feel like an idiot half the time.

LEO: That it's democratizing.

VERA: What?

LEO: That with the internet, information is free to everyone, it um . . . de-commodifies knowledge. Which is power.

(He returns to his yellow page search.)

VERA: When you put it that way I think I should learn how to use the computer.

LEO: Marx is cool.

VERA: You think so?

LEO: He's all right.

VERA: Well I think so, too.

LEO: When I did that semester at Evergreen I took a class on Marx. Best class I took.

VERA: What did your mother think of that?

LEO: About me studying Marx?

VERA: Yeah.

LEO: Uh, I think she was like, "How is that going to be useful to you, in the future?"

VERA: Oh, dear.

LEO: And I was like, first of all, who knows, and second, I think it's important to understand where I come from, which is where you come from, too, so I'm surprised you aren't more supportive.

VERA *(Delighted)*: You said that?

LEO: I did.

VERA: And what did she say?

LEO: You know, as long as I was in college, she was happy, so I think she just shut up.

VERA: She and I don't talk about politics anymore. I always end up telling her how disappointing she was to her father, I don't mean to, somehow or other I just wind up saying it, and I only mean in terms of the political—not *generally*, but then she starts crying and going on about how she always votes Democrat, as if that's . . . it's better we just don't talk about it.

LEO: I find that to be true about a lot of subjects with Jane.

VERA: Well, between you and me. I guess I do, too.

(A small moment of enjoying each other.)

But she was always my favorite because she was the littlest, you know she was only two when Joe and I started carrying on together. And she's been very devoted to me, so.

LEO: Is 23rd Street pretty near here?

VERA: Matter of fact you can walk there. I guess I should get you Joe's keys.

LEO: Um—

(She doesn't hear him and exits. He prepares himself to ask for something. She reenters with keys.)

VERA: I better show you which one does what, and you'll get it wrong the first few times anyway but you'll eventually learn.

LEO: Okay—I was wondering if you could spot me a few bucks? For climbing?

VERA: Oh. You're out of money, is that it?

LEO: At the moment the flow is low.

VERA: How much do you need?

LEO: I don't know what prices are like around here . . . I have to rent all the stuff, so like, fifty?

VERA: Fifty *dollars*?

LEO: That's what it would be in Seattle, so I guess . . . maybe a little more?

VERA: More than *fifty* dollars? To climb up a wall?

LEO: I'm expecting an influx in a couple days so I could pay / you back.

VERA: A what?

LEO: An influx! Of cash, into my account!

VERA: From where?

From your mother? She's still giving you money? Well . . .

LEO: Forget it.

VERA: No, / listen—

LEO: Forget it! It's no big deal!

VERA: I'm going to show you where I keep the money, and then when you need some you can just take it and leave a note, all right? So I know how much you took and I won't worry about it.

All right?

LEO: All right.

VERA: And then maybe you can do some shopping, and get the things around the house you like to have for breakfast and so on and so forth.

LEO: Vera, I want to be really clear that I can't stay more than a couple days.

VERA: I understand.

LEO: It's great to rest up, but I need to make it back to Washington before it gets too cold, so.

VERA: You mean, on the bike?

LEO: Yup.

VERA: You're going to go all the way back west on that bike?

LEO: That's the plan.

(An uncomprehending pause.)

VERA: Maybe if you called Rebecca today, she—since it was the middle of the night, she may not / have—

LEO: It's not / about—

VERA: Seeing as you came all this way to be with her—

LEO: I didn't.

I didn't come all this way to be with her.

VERA: Well I know it wasn't to be with *me*.

LEO: It was to finish something I started. Micah and I started something. I finished it. That's it. People want to make it really complicated but it's not.

(He gives her a big smile.)

VERA: If you stayed more than a couple days I wouldn't know what to say to your mother. I don't know what to say to her as it is. So we're in agreement.

I keep the money in Joe's study.

(She tries to stand, doesn't quite make it up, winds up and stands again. She makes her way out slowly. Leo stays seated. He is fending off a wave of nausea or vertigo.)

(Calling off) You comin' or what?

Scene 3

A few days later.
> *Leo is lying down, eating something and reading a book.*
> *The sound of a key in the lock.*
> *It takes a long time for Vera to get the door open.*
> *She enters slowly, more off balance than usual. She is wearing dark clothing.*
> *She sees Leo, who waves and goes back to reading.*

VERA: Did you lock the top lock?
LEO: No.
VERA: Are you sure?
LEO: Yup.

> *(She turns and looks at the door, perplexed.)*

VERA: Well I think you must have and then forgotten.
LEO: I haven't touched the door today, Vera.
VERA: Maybe you did it without really thinking about it.

LEO: Uh, okay, sure, I for no reason / and without thinking—
VERA: You have to speak louder if you want me to hear you.
LEO: I didn't lock the top lock!
VERA: Well . . . *(Flustered)* all right.
LEO: Does it really matter?
VERA: I made sure I didn't lock it when I left, because it's getting harder for me to hold the, whaddayacallit, the—*key*, because my hand shakes, which is disgusting, but then it was locked anyway so either you did it or I'm going crazy, which I must admit is very possible.

(She exits toward the bedroom, upset. He sits up. He thinks of going after her, then lies back down and continues reading. She reenters.)

I don't mind if you break something, accidents happen, but nothing drives me crazier than when somebody breaks something and doesn't tell me.

(She exits again.)

LEO: What did I break? Vera?

(He puts the book down and begins to follow her but she reenters on her way to the kitchen.)

What did I break?
VERA: Never mind, just tell me next time, all right?
LEO: Dude, I have no idea what you're talking about.
VERA: Now you're really making me mad.
LEO: Tell me what I did!

(She looks at him with disbelief.)

VERA: The faucet! In your bathroom?

(He thinks hard.)

LEO: The faucet . . .

VERA: Oh, gimme a break!

LEO: You gotta help me out here, Grandma.

VERA: The whaddayacallit, the . . .

LEO: The whaddayacallit.

VERA: Don't make fun of me!

LEO: I'm not!

VERA: The . . . handle, that you turn. It's completely off.

LEO: I thought it was always like that.

(She shoots him an accusing look.)

I did!

VERA: No, it wasn't "always like that." I went in there to clean this morning while you were still asleep because it was filthy, because you obviously haven't cleaned since you've been here, and that was the first time I ever saw it like that.

LEO: It came right off in my hand, I swear I thought—

VERA: Well, just tell me, is all I'm asking, I don't think that's an unreasonable request, do you?

(She exits into the kitchen. Pause.)

LEO *(Calling off)*: Sorry!

(Loud noises come from the kitchen. Leo decides not to take this on. He lies back down and keeps reading. After a few moments she reenters, still in a state.)

VERA: In case you're interested, I just came from a funeral, so that's where I've been all morning.

LEO: Okay.

119

VERA: It was for the last of the octogenarians.

LEO: The what?

VERA: There were seven of us, octogenarians, and we had dinner once a month for a lot of years and we were all lefties and there were a lot of memories and laughs and the last one just died, besides me.

LEO: Sorry.

VERA: Yeah, he was a rat, very aggressive, he used to make passes at me with his wife sitting right there. She had Alzheimer's so she didn't mind, but I did. Even so, he was the last one and I don't feel very happy about it.

LEO: You want a hug from a hippie?

VERA: No, I'm all right.

(She goes back into the kitchen. A moment later she reenters. Leo goes to her and hugs her.)

And I spoke to your mother this morning, too. And I did not tell her you're here, even though you were all she talked about, and she's really, whaddayacallit, in distress, and I'm not feeling terribly proud of myself.

(He separates.)

LEO: You can't take all that on. You have to let her find her own way.

VERA: Well see, that's not how I think about things. Because I believe in a . . . a society where . . . here I go with my words. The point is you help people, it's about the community, it's not about I do what's best for me and you do what's best for you, because . . . you know the one thing I wasn't thinking when Joe was dying was I better pay attention to what he says, about politics, because I always relied on him to, to make the arguments, and explain the . . .

(She shakes her head, lost, disgusted with herself.)

LEO *(Gently)*: I've been reading this book he edited, about Cuba?

VERA: Oh, yeah?

LEO: It's really interesting. I didn't know this stuff, about their health-care system—

VERA: Oh, their health care is wonderful. And literacy, too.

LEO: Grandpa's introduction is really . . . I don't remember him that well? You know? But I remember his voice, he had / that—

VERA: Yes.

LEO: Yeah, so I've been imagining his voice reading this, and it's like . . . so sure?

VERA: Indeed.

LEO: The way he writes, it's . . . it almost reads as a little hokey, now, because it's so—but I think it must have been cool, to be so, um. Uncynical. Like I think I'm really uncynical, and Micah was definitely totally uncynical, but *you* guys. That's like a whole other level of . . . I'm definitely learning about Grandpa. It's definitely cool.

(Pause.)

VERA: Your mother told me something very upsetting about you this morning that I have been debating bringing up with you at all. Do you want to know what it is?

LEO: Not really.

VERA: She said in the beginning of the summer, when you were home for a little while in St. / Paul—

LEO: Oh my *God*, she's / still—

VERA: That you tried to kiss your sister.

LEO: I cannot *believe* she is still fixated on that!

VERA: Well that was pretty disturbing for Lily, I would think.

LEO: It was—we were all—it was so *not* disturbing, she was not disturbed, and *tried* is not really the—I mean, we kissed, lots of people were kissing, it was like a spontaneous kissing convention, and we kissed, and it was so not a big deal except for in our totally taboo / laden—

VERA: Well she's in therapy about it now is all I'm saying.

LEO: I cannot—! Okay. Okay. Fine. She's in therapy, because we were both fucked on peyote and we kissed, *once*, with totally minimal tongue, and *not* because our parents are obsessed with the fact that they *don't treat her differently* just because she's adopted and never fail to mention that to her for a single day in her life. *Obviously* it was the totally harmless and even I would say pleasant smooch that sent her reeling into identity confusion. I mean, it's not like I fucked / her.

VERA: She's your sister!

LEO: Yeah! And she's awesome! And I wish she would get the fuck out of that house!

VERA: You need to learn how to take some responsibility, you know that? You're right, I've seen the way they are about the—the fact is, they didn't think they would be able to have you, when they adopted her, and—there's a guilt there, and a nervousness, but—you're a sensitive young man and you should be able to understand that and not be so angry about it. And you should be able to understand that she's vulnerable, she always has been, and kissing her wasn't the best idea. That's all. That's all.

LEO: It's just . . . it's hard to think of something more emblematic of our society, that a kiss expressing real mutual love between two people is considered destructive.

VERA: You know better than that.

LEO: I don't, Grandma, and I don't want to.

(Pause.)

122

VERA: Rebecca found out about it, is that it? And that's why she's so mad?

LEO: Bec knows about it, because she was there, and she *also* kissed Lily, incidentally, which was really beautiful, and no, she is not mad, because she's way more open-minded than that.

VERA: And I'm old and closed-minded, is that it?

LEO: You're old, but you could choose not to be closed-minded.

(He goes back to his book.)

VERA: You didn't say anything about the buzzer.

LEO: The what?

VERA: I had the super change the name on the buzzer, since you didn't seem to be getting around to it. It has my name now. Only took me ten years, but it has my name now.

LEO: Uh . . . congratulations? Sorry, is that—what am I supposed to say?

(Pause. He goes back to his book.)

VERA: Well.

(She stands slowly to go. She exits into the kitchen.)

123

Scene 4

Lights up on Bec. She is not chubby. She is in fact strong and beauti-
ful and hale, though she is also somewhat strung-out. She may wear
a puffy vest over a sweater. She may wear hiking boots. She may
have a Nalgene bottle.

    She stands uncomfortably for a long time. Vera enters, walking
slowly with a cup of tea. She sees Bec is still standing.

VERA: Take a load off.

> *(Bec sits. Vera very gingerly, shakily, places the tea in front of*
> *her. She thinks of something.)*

You take sugar?
BEC *(She does)*: Oh—no—

> *(Vera sees through this and frowningly exits for sugar. Bec drops*
> *her head in her hands. Silence. Vera returns, slowly, with a*
> *sugar bowl and a few packets of Sweet'N Low.)*

VERA: My neighbor across the hall is a diabetic, so I keep this
  stuff around. In case you watch that sort of thing.
BEC: Thank you.

*(Bec helps herself to two heaping spoonfuls of sugar while Vera
watches disapprovingly.)*

You don't have to—if you have something else you need
  to do—
VERA: You want me to leave you alone, is that it?
BEC: No, just, I don't want you to feel you have to, like—
VERA: What?
BEC: I don't want to be in your way!
VERA: Well, you're not. Particularly.

(Vera sits as well. They don't know what to say to each other.)

So you're having second thoughts, is that it?
BEC: What?
  No, I . . . no.

(Another silence.)

VERA: When I was first married. Not to Joe, to my first hus-
  band, Arthur. It was a week or two we had been married
  and a woman showed up at our apartment with luggage.
  Arthur said to me, "Oh I forgot to tell you, before we were
  married I promised I would take her away for the week-
  end and I didn't want to fink on a promise." *(Bec horrified,
  Vera laughing)* So I said all right, and they went away, and
  I left my key on the piano and went home to my parents.
BEC: And you divorced him?
VERA: Oh no. He came to my parents at the end of the week-
  end begging and pleading and I thought it was funny that
  he had been so stupid so I went home with him. It wasn't
  the last time he cheated.

125

BEC: Of course not!

VERA: When we had been married six months he went out to Hollywood with a woman . . . oh God, what was her name. She was rich, and neurotic. *Muriel.* He and Muriel went out there to write a screenplay and her father bankrolled them and Arthur never sent me a penny. And I guess they were having an affair because when he tried to end it she threatened to kill herself, and that was a terrible mess. One time we were all at Café Society . . .

I guess they were back from California . . . ?

And she followed me into a cab and said, "Can't we be friends? It eats away at me that you're angry at me," and so forth. And I said, "Listen, Muriel, there are people you like and people you don't, and I don't like you, and I want you out of this cab." And she cried and carried on, this woman who had been sleeping with my husband for two years . . .

(Long pause. Bec drinks her tea.)

Then there was the waitress he met in Arkansas. And he came home and confessed he was in love with her, and I said, "Listen, she's a hick, you have nothing in common, I'm sure the sex is terrific and whatnot but why don't you go back there and spend a few weeks with her and see if there's really enough there for you to leave our marriage." And he did. And sure enough he came back and said, "You're right, we ran out of things to talk about." And that was that.

He was a cheater and a drunk, but I liked him till the day he died.

BEC *(Blurting it out)*: I'm not sure what you're trying to tell me.

VERA: What?

BEC: I don't know what you want me to—why are you telling me this?

VERA: I was just making conversation. I wasn't getting much help from you.

BEC: But you're going on and on about these—like, parables of tolerance and forgiveness—you should have left him!

VERA: I did, eventually.

BEC: But you put up with like—and you tell these stories like you're proud of them.

VERA (*Seeing that Bec is truly upset*): Okay, listen—

BEC: This woman, who you tried to push out of a cab, you should have pushed *him* out of a cab, she was coming to you / for understanding—

VERA: I see I've struck a / nerve.

BEC: I'm not going to forgive him!

VERA: All right. All right.

(*Bec struggling to get control, Vera totally unsure what to do.*)

BEC: I'm sorry, I've been really . . .

And I can't believe he's fucking late, I can't *believe* . . .

VERA: Listen, I wasn't trying to say forgive him or don't forgive him. I don't know what you should do, that's your affair.

I was trying to say . . . men sometimes do things that can be very . . . but you have to remember that it's more out of stupidity than anything else. It's not, whaddayacallit. Malicious. It's just stupid and childish.

BEC: I guess, um . . . (*Searching for the inoffensive way to say this*) I don't make those kinds of allowances, based on gender? I wouldn't want anyone to make those kinds of allowances for me, so . . .

VERA: I suppose you think I'm very backward.

BEC: No—

(*The sound of a key in the lock. Bec hears it immediately and prepares herself, Vera looks around suspiciously to see what she heard. Leo enters, his pants covered in dirt. Both women look at him. He grins.)*

LEO: I found a community garden.

(Vera winds up and stands.)

VERA: Excuse me.

(She exits into her bedroom slowly. Leo heads in for a kiss, Bec dodges him.)

BEC: I told you I have class at two.
LEO: Am I late?
BEC: I can't miss any more class.
LEO: I said I'd come up to you.
BEC: And I said I didn't want you in my apartment.

(He grins.)

LEO: I brought you something.

(He produces a small, sad, dirty pumpkin from his hoodie pocket. He approaches her very slowly and extends it to her. She takes it.)

BEC: What do you want me to do with this, Leo?
LEO: Love it. Nurture it. Teach it what you know.
    Make a pie.

(She throws it back at him. He catches it. It is unclear whether some of the tension is broken or if she is angrier than ever.)

I miss you all the time. I think of you in *college*. I think about whether they have left-handed desks for you.

BEC: They do.

LEO: That's good.

BEC: Sometimes right-handed people sit at the left-handed desks and I get really pissed.

LEO: Bastards.

BEC: Yeah. I'm like, you're not just hurting me, you're hurting yourself.

(They smile. This is their thing.)

LEO: You like it?

BEC: I don't want to talk about college with you, Leo.

LEO: Why not?

BEC: Because you're just gonna be, like, disdainful.

LEO: I'm not!

I wanna hear.

BEC: It's . . . I don't know, everyone's so much younger than me, I mean just two years, but it seems like . . . so it's lonely. But I'm taking this class on global health that I think is really . . . I met with the professor a couple times and I might help her with some research next summer in Mumbai, if the money works out.

LEO: Man, you work fast.

BEC: I walked into her office and I was like, "I've built houses in Ecuador and taught English in Mali and installed solar panels in Kathmandu and I want to know how I can work with you."

And she was like, "Wow, it's so refreshing to meet a female undergraduate who doesn't end every sentence in a question mark."

So . . .

LEO: You always wanted to go to India.

BEC: It'll be so nice to travel somewhere not on my parents' dime, you know?

LEO: I could come.

129

BEC: . . . to Mumbai?

LEO: Why not?

(Pause.)

BEC: I want to break up.   LEO: I'm so happy to see you.

LEO: Whoa. Oh. Okay.

(Pause.)

Okay.

(He grins at her.)

BEC: The other night when I said I needed some time to think, that wasn't true, I want to break up. Sorry, I know the timing is shitty. I was gonna do it no matter what when you finished the bike trip, it's not . . . it's not about you going AWOL this summer, even though I'm really fucking pissed about that.

LEO: So you—huh. You were planning this for a while.

BEC: Yeah. Yes.

LEO: That's why you backed out of the bike trip.

BEC: Ummmmm . . . no, I backed out of the bike trip because I—I didn't *back out* of the bike trip, I was never definitely coming on the bike trip.

LEO: Uh, okay, I remember it differently but it really doesn't matter now, so.

BEC: You knew I was applying for internships, you knew that.

LEO: Yeah, and I knew you were buying gear and training and, like, telling me you loved me and it was important we got to spend this time together before you left for school. That's all.

BEC: Well when Allison backed out—

LEO: Allison tore her ACL, dude, that's / totally—

BEC: Fine, but it wasn't gonna be the trip we'd planned, it wasn't gonna be the four of us.

LEO: But you admit that we had *planned* a trip, you *planned* to come with us, that was the *plan*. But I guess you were already *planning* to break up with me, you just didn't let me in on that.

BEC: I'm sorry I didn't come on the bike trip, okay?

LEO: No, it was good, it was amazing, actually, to have that time with Micah, so. I wouldn't trade that for anything.

BEC: Well good.

(Brief pause.)

LEO: I mean, it would have been nice to have you there when he was killed, it would have been nice to not be alone for that.

BEC: Yeah, it would have been nice if you'd showed up at the funeral, I really needed you then. Do you know how hurtful that was, and humiliating, that everyone was like, "Where the fuck is Leo?" And I was like, "I don't know, he hasn't even *called me*."

LEO: But you were already planning to break up with me. *(Off her look)* What? I'm just, I'm trying to master this time line, Bec, it's a little confusing.

BEC: You're laying this all on me, but we had problems. We never had the kind of relationship Micah and Allison had, I think we should just face that.

LEO: We—? I don't even know what that means.

BEC: They were like actual grown-ups in love, like really in love. I'm not saying we didn't love each other—

LEO: No, you're saying I'm not a grown-up.

BEC: I'm saying—even my mom still talks about it, what a mature, and, like, evenly balanced—

LEO: Oh, well, if *Ellen* / thought so—

131

BEC: Don't be an asshole, you know what I mean, they just had this serenity that we—

LEO: I actually thought it was the other way around, that we were the ones with the real deal because I thought about you basically all the time when you weren't there and talked about you like some kind of pathetic lovesick idiot whereas Micah never thought about Ally at all.

BEC: That's because he didn't have to.

(Brief pause.)

LEO: I think you have some very weird very idealized picture of their relationship, because it might interest you to know that he cheated on her, actually.

BEC: Okay.

LEO: Like several times. With some extremely questionable specimens.

BEC: It's not cheating when it's an open relationship and it's really none of my business and I don't think it's cool at all to talk about him that way.

LEO: I just think it's interesting that your idea of a perfect relationship involves your boyfriend getting a BJ from the fifteen-year-old girl whose uncle owns the campground.

BEC: My idea of the perfect relationship involves feeling like I don't have to justify myself all the fucking time to someone who claims that they love me but is constantly disappointed in me. I am so tired of disappointing you, Leo.

And fuck you for telling me that about Micah, I did not want to know that.

(Vera has entered with a laundry cart.)

VERA: Excuse me. I was going to the basement to do some laundry, I wondered if you have anything that needs to be washed.

LEO: No.

VERA: Are you sure? I haven't washed your sheets since you've / been here.

LEO: No!

    Thanks.

(Vera exits slowly, with dignity.)

BEC: You know Micah's parents are back together, right?

LEO: . . . *what?*

BEC: I know.

LEO: Oh, no.

BEC: I actually tried to talk to them about it, I was like, you know I love you both, but is this really a good idea? For you guys, and for Ethan? It was so weird, I felt like such an adult.

LEO: What did they say?

BEC: He cried, and told me how proud he is of me, and how lucky Micah was to have me in his life, and she got super huffy and passive-aggressive and they both assured me that it's what Micah would have wanted. Which seems to me both patently false and completely irrelevant.

LEO: They're gonna destroy that poor kid.

BEC: And he's such a / sweet kid.

LEO: He's a good kid. He / really is.

BEC: It's a shit show, I give up.

(Pause.)

    I gotta get back uptown.

LEO: Hold on, I want to read you something.

BEC: Leo, I'm already late.

LEO: It's short.

(He exits, then returns with a book of Rumi poetry. He takes a few moments to find the page.)

133

"There Is a Field."
That's the title.
BEC: Leo—
LEO: You have to promise to listen with an open heart.
BEC: I—
LEO: Please.

(She breathes, tries impatiently but earnestly to listen with an open heart.)

(Reading)
Out beyond ideas of wrongdoing and rightdoing there
is a field.

(He swallows. This is hard for him.)

I'll meet you there.
When the soul lies down in that grass
The world is too full to talk about.

(Pause. She sees he is almost overcome, puts a hand on him. He takes the opportunity to grab her and kiss her. She pushes him away.)

BEC: I have to go.
LEO: Let me touch you.
BEC: No.
LEO: You're forgetting how our bodies are together.
BEC: No I'm not.

(She gently disentangles and moves away.)

When I'm not furious at you I'm really worried about you. I don't want you to become someone who makes me sad every time I think about you.

LEO: Okay, Bec, I'll go to *college.*

BEC: Fuck you.

LEO: One of us has turned our back on everything the four of us used to believe and it isn't me.

(Vera reenters from the hall, without the cart but carrying detergent. Bec gathers her stuff angrily, tearfully, while Leo looks at the ground.)

Hey.

(He extends the pumpkin toward Bec, smiling idiotically. Bec ignores him and walks past Vera out the door without speaking. A silence.)

VERA: Well.

Are you all right?

LEO: Yeah, I'm good.

VERA: She's lost weight.

(Pause.)

She could lose / some more—

LEO *(Quietly)*: Shut up.

VERA: What?

LEO *(With his grin, loudly)*: It makes me sick to hear you talk about her body, so just fucking stop, okay? Did you hear that?

(She is stunned. He exits into the bedroom.)

Scene 5

Several days later, around dusk. Leo and Vera sit, staring out into space. Something is different, though we don't know right away what it is. A silence.

VERA: Weren't you on a sailboat for a while?
LEO: Yeah. Yeah. In Mexico.

   (Pause.)

VERA: And he was there? What's-his-name.

   (Pause.)

   Micah.
LEO: Yeah. He was there.

   (Pause.)

And Ally was there too, for a while, but she got hepatitis
and had to be evac-ed back to St. Paul.

VERA: Hepatitis? What were you eating?

LEO: Fish, mostly. Rice.

VERA: You caught the fish?

LEO: Yeah, with a, like. Harpoon kinda thing. You shoot them
with this spear thing.

VERA: Aren't they fast?

LEO: Yeah.

VERA: Isn't it hard to hit them?

LEO: Yeah. They're fast. Micah was good at it.

(Pause.)

And the spear has a flotation device so after they're speared
they rise to the surface.

(Pause.)

VERA: What does?

LEO: What?

VERA: I forget what we were talking about.

(Pause. Pause.)

LEO: Me, too.

(More staring.)

VERA: You know your father never did anything for me in bed.

(Pause.)

LEO: *What?* My father?

VERA: Yeah. Joe.

LEO: Joe was my grandfather.
VERA: Oh. Right.

(Leo giggles.)

Well he never did anything for me in bed. Neither of my husbands did. There was only one man who ever did anything for me in bed and it wasn't one of the ones I married.
LEO: Who was it?
VERA: My lips are sealed.
LEO: I won't tell.
VERA: Nope. Taking it with me to the grave.

(Pause.)

LEO: I've been incredibly horny since Micah died.

(Pause.)

VERA: Sure.

(Pause.)

LEO: Bec has kind of a weird pussy. But I like it.
        Did you hear me?
VERA: Yes, but I don't want to discuss it.

*(Pause.
        Leo picks up a bowl and lighter that we haven't noticed from the table.)*

LEO: You want some more?
VERA: No thank you, I didn't like the way it made my throat . . .
        Whaddayacallit.

(He lights and pulls.)

And I don't think it's really doing anything for me, besides.

LEO *(Holding the smoke in his lungs)*: Were my parents ever in love?

(He exhales.)

VERA: Which ones are your parents? Oh right.

(She thinks.)

I never really understood your father. He's not very. Whaddayacallit.

(She thinks.)

Forthcoming. He doesn't . . .

LEO: Come forth?

(They both laugh.)

VERA: You know, your mother was always nervous. About . . . stupid things. She always thought she had offended someone, and then when she thinks that, she starts acting peculiar and she does offend people.
   What was the question?

LEO: Were my parents ever in love?

VERA: I think at first he made her stop worrying, and now he makes her worry more. But that's just what I think, and that and a dollar fifty will get me on the subway.

(Pause.)

LEO: Biggest regret?

VERA: Maybe I would have liked to have one of my own children. I didn't know I wanted one until I married Joe and his kids were around and then I thought, that would have been nice, to have one from the very beginning instead of coming in late like that.

(Pause.)

LEO: Thank you for celebrating the autumnal equinox with me this way.

(She nods.)

Scene 6

In blackness, the sound of a key in the lock. Sound of a young woman giggling.

The door opens and light spills into the apartment from the hall. The giggling gets louder. Leo enters with a drunk Amanda leaning on him. He turns on a light. Amanda is young looking for nineteen—a pretty and fashion-forward Chinese-American woman. She alternately giggles and says, "Shhhhhh!"

LEO: It's okay, she's deaf.

AMANDA: Really? That's so sad!

LEO: You want a drink?

AMANDA: Yeah, what do you have?

LEO *(With the liquor cabinet)*: Uh . . . Campari?

AMANDA: This view is amaaaaaaaazing!

LEO: Uh, something that the label is too old to read . . .

AMANDA: I can't believe you live here. Do you just wake up every morning and think I can't believe I live here?

LEO: Not really.

AMANDA: What does she pay?

LEO: I dunno, I think she said like around twelve hundred.

(Amanda screams.)

Shhhhh!

AMANDA *(Whispering)*: Are you *serious*? Do you know how much my apartment costs?

LEO: I don't.

AMANDA: Eighteen hundred! It's about the size of this room! How long has she been here?

LEO: I don't know.

AMANDA *(Back with the view)*: This is south, right?

LEO: Uh . . .

AMANDA: Did she watch the towers fall?

LEO: I have no idea.

AMANDA: You don't ask her nearly enough questions. If she was my grandma I'd know everything. I'm like obsessed with family history. If you want to know the names of all my great-grandmother's siblings in Chural Rina I'll . . .

(She cracks up.)

Rural. China. I'm drunk. Are you drunk?

(Leo pours two Camparis.)

LEO: I wasn't drinking.

AMANDA: You *weren't*? Are you gonna like date-rape me?

LEO *(Nervous)*: Uh . . .

AMANDA: I'm just kidding, I'll totally sleep with you. I mean probably. I like you. You're like a mountain man. Like a real live mountain man. Of the mountains. You live out-side of society's, like . . .

(She can't think of how to finish the sentence. He hands her a Campari.)

LEO: I don't really know what this is, but it matches your Band-Aid.

AMANDA: Oh, yeah!

(She lifts a pinky finger, revealing a bright pink/orange Band-Aid.)

Did I tell you how I got this?

LEO: No.

AMANDA: I totally shut my finger in a cab door! If I showed you you wouldn't believe it, it's like nine colors. I might not have a pinky fingernail ever again!

LEO: That's good, it's like your signature. Like your original thing.

AMANDA: But I'm already like a total freak, I mean look at me.

LEO: I don't think you're a freak.

AMANDA *(Disappointed)*: You don't?

LEO *(Backtracking)*: I mean—

AMANDA: I'm just teasing you, I'm just kidding. You're adorable, you're so cute.

LEO: I wanna see under it.

AMANDA: Under what? My Band-Aid?

LEO: Yeah, I wanna see the colors.

AMANDA: Ew! Gross! No! I mean, not *yet*.

(She drinks some of the Campari.)

Wow, this is nasty.

LEO: Sorry, I can—

AMANDA: No, in a good way.

(A flirtatious pause. He leans in for the kiss. She ducks coquettishly away and goes back to the window.)

So what's your deal, mountain man?

LEO: My—?

AMANDA: I'll tell you my deal first, that's only fair. I'm at Parsons, duh. I sort of have a boyfriend but mostly not right now. I grew up in San Francisco, my parents run like a dim sum empire, so I'm kinda rich and I don't really like to apologize for it. Um, my sister is five years older and she already has two kids which I think is so gross. Like I can't even stand to be in her house because of the smell. And I'm gonna be an international art star, that much is clear, though I don't know exactly what medium yet.

Your turn.

LEO: Um, I'm from St. Paul. And . . . now I'm here, by way of Seattle.

(Brief pause.)

AMANDA: Wow, you're really, like, milking this man of few words, romantic scruffy beard thing.

LEO: I just really want to kiss you, Amelia.

AMANDA: Am / anda.

LEO: Amanda! Sorry! I knew I was gonna do that.

AMANDA: Yeah, that just set you back, like, at least twenty minutes.

LEO: Amanda Amanda Amanda Amanda Amanda.

AMANDA: You should do that inside your head instead of out loud.

LEO: Sorry.

AMANDA: Your name is Leo, which means Lion. What's your astrological sign?

LEO: Not Leo. Virgo.

AMANDA: Mine's Libra. *(She mimes scales)* Balance.

LEO: You're really beautiful, Amanda.

AMANDA: That's good, keep practicing my name, soon you won't even have to think about it.

LEO: I'm sorry, I'm really not an asshole.

AMANDA: Who's Amelia. Ex-girlfriend?

LEO: No, I—don't take this the wrong way, but I think I did that because all night I was afraid I was gonna call you Lily? Which is my sister's name? You sorta remind me of her.

AMANDA *(A joke)*: Is she Chinese?

LEO: Yeah.

AMANDA: Seriously?

LEO: Yeah, she's adopted.

AMANDA: And she's an amazing dresser? No, that's a joke. But seriously, is she?

LEO: No, she's much more, like . . . Banana Republic than you.

AMANDA: Ooh.

LEO: But it's just, something in the . . . *(He gestures vaguely toward his face)* I dunno.

AMANDA: That's sweet, mountain man. I think that's really sweet. Where is she?

LEO: St. Paul. With my parents. She was in college, but then she took a semester off, and now it's like her third year off, and she's not really sure what she's doing. I'm kinda worried about her.

AMANDA: What's she good at?

LEO: She has the most amazing voice in the world. She sounds like a songbird, I know that's a fucking cliché, but if you were in the woods and you heard her singing, you would seriously think it was like the most talented bird you had ever heard.

AMANDA: You miss her.

LEO: Yeah.

AMANDA: Why are you here?

LEO: Well, my grandma's really old, and she doesn't really have anybody, so. I thought it would be cool to come spend some time with her.

AMANDA: That is *so sweet*!

LEO: I don't really see it that way, as, like, a favor? She's just a like a really good friend who I happen to be related to.

AMANDA: You might be too good to be true, new friend. You might be.

(He moves slowly toward her. She dodges him and goes to the bookshelf.)

I don't know why I'm feeling kind of shy, it's uncharacteristic, I'm usually pretty slutty.
    (With a book) Is your grandmother like a communist?

LEO: Card carrying.

AMANDA *(Alarmed)*: Seriously?!

LEO: Yeah. Why?

AMANDA: Oh my God. Oh my God. I'm sorry. I like, *hate*. Communists.

LEO: What? Why?

AMANDA: Duh! I'm Chinese! Why do you think my family left?

LEO: Oh.

AMANDA: Why do you think your *sister* was put up for *adoption*? Because the communists like fucked China up the ass!

LEO: Um, I'm not sure if / that's—

AMANDA: Oh it is. That is *literally* what happened.

LEO: Okay . . . sorry?

AMANDA: Are *you* a communist?

LEO: Um . . . no.

AMANDA: You had to think about that.

(He tries to kiss her again.)

Dude! I'm not sure I can get it on in a communist's apartment, I'm really not.

LEO: A lot of people were communists back then—it was like, it was like . . . recycling, or whatever.

AMANDA: What?

LEO: Like it was cool, it was something you did to be, you know, responsible. To society. I'm not a communist, I swear, I'm not.

AMANDA *(Seriously)*: My family didn't do so well over there, okay? I know I'm like this funny weird girl in platform shoes, but I actually am not joking at all and would get really upset if I told you what happened.

(Long pause.)

LEO: My best friend died this summer.

(She looks at him.)

We were biking across the country together and he died. That's why I'm here. Because I don't know where else to be.
      Amanda.

(A long pause. She grabs his face. They kiss passionately. Vera enters, disoriented. She doesn't have her teeth in so her lips curl over her gums. They don't hear her and continue, with hands moving all over each other. She sees what's going on, startles slightly, and then realizes what she's looking at. She turns to go, but Amanda, in a moment of pulling away and opening her eyes, sees her and screams. They separate.)

AMANDA: Oh my God!
VERA *(Holding up a hand)*: Excuse me.

(She exits.)

AMANDA: Oh my *God*! That scared the *shit* out of me! She looked like a ghost! She looked like a little white-haired old lady ghost!

LEO: Here, come to my room.

AMANDA: Hold on, that really freaked me out!

LEO: Okay, okay.

(She goes to sit on the couch. He tentatively sits near her and rubs her back.)

It's cool. She doesn't care.

AMANDA: I don't want to get old and lose all my teeth, that shit is so *fucked*.

LEO: Shhhhhhh.

(He continues to rub her back. She begins to relax. He moves in a little closer.)

AMANDA: What was your friend's name?

(Brief pause.)

LEO: Micah.

AMANDA: How did he die?

(He stops rubbing her back.)

Sorry.

LEO: No, you're right, the old lady kinda killed the mood.

(Long pause.)

AMANDA: God, is tomorrow Tuesday?

LEO: I'm not sure.

AMANDA: I actually have class really early, I totally forgot that.
I know it sounds like a lame excuse, but it's actually true.

LEO: It's fine.

AMANDA: Are you gonna have blue balls or anything?

LEO: No.

AMANDA: I feel kinda bad.

LEO: Don't.

AMANDA: I could give you my number? . . .

(He doesn't respond.)

Ohhhhh*kay.*

LEO: I just, I probably wouldn't use it? So . . .

(She stands. She's not sure what to do, so she just walks to the door. She has trouble with the lock. He goes to the door and unlocks it. She turns to him, angry, ashamed.)

AMANDA: I'm glad I didn't let you see under my Band-Aid.

(She exits.)

Scene 7

The middle of the night. Leo is sitting in darkness.
  Vera enters in her nightgown and turns on a light. Seeing Leo,
she turns it off. It's actually dark as opposed to "stage dark" so that
we can only see their silhouettes against the window. She goes and
sits near him. A silence.

LEO: So we were in Kansas, because—even though that was
    way out of the way we wanted to hit the center of the
    country, preferably around the Fourth of July for maxi-
    mum earnestness slash unacknowledged irony factor.
    The timing worked out so it was July 3rd and we were
    approaching Gypsum, our small town America of choice,
    one bar, one diner, seventeen churches or whatever. And
    we were going west to east, so, wind at our backs. The
    wind comes out of the south in the summer, but more like
    the southwest, so in a way going west to east was a pussy
    move on our parts, but we kind of wanted to do the oppo-
    site of the historical—like American is east to west, so we

were going the opposite way, also we lived out west, so. It was more honest to start there.

Western Kansas is like ass flat, the cliché, so you're basically just riding the wind and if you pedal even a little bit in a low gear you hit fifteen mph no problem. Fifteen mph is a slow speed in a car, but on a bike it's pretty good, it's pretty good. So it's morning and the sun's pretty low; between the low sun and the flat ride and the good wind it's the perfect time to take shadow pictures. That means you take a picture of your own shadow while you're riding, totally a staple of the cross country bike trip, gotta have the shadow picture, and with our huge packs and panniers we were gonna have especially dope shadow pictures. Micah thinks he's a really good photographer, he thinks he has talent, so he's doing a lot of bullshit with shutter speed and framing and what have you and we're both taking shadow pictures and we hear a truck coming behind us, or I hear it, I assume Micah does, I think he does because we both hug the shoulder a little bit, still taking our shadow shots, and the truck gets louder and closer and passes us and I see it's a Tyson truck full of fucking crates of screaming chickens packed together and there are feathers flying out of the truck bed like some kind of I don't know what kind of metaphor, and I scream up to Micah who did I mention was in front of me, look at that fucking slave poultry! And he looks back at me, he has his left hand on his handlebar and his right hand still on his bullshit professional camera and he looks back at me and he's laughing and he starts to say something but the truck bed separates from the cab and flies backward and takes him off the road.

(Silence, save for city sounds.)

Before the ambulance came this PR lady from Tyson came. I didn't realize I was still holding my camera. She was like, "I'm sorry, sir, but I have to confiscate your camera." She has to yell it for me to hear her over all these maimed and freaked-out birds. I was like, "My best friend is under three thousand chickens." She was like, "I understand you're upset, but this will be easier for both of us if you just give me your camera now." I was like, "I couldn't get to him, he's buried under there, where is the fucking ambulance?" And she was like, "I'm going to ask you one more time—" and I threw my camera on the ground.

(Silence.)

So what I don't have is these pictures from Wyoming, we did these stupid corny timer shots at the top of the Continental Divide, in front of the sign that says the altitude and all that shit, there was still snow up there in June. He caught a fish in Yellowstone, with his bare hands, he stood really still and reached in and . . . I had a picture of him holding up this fish longer than his head and neck. Oh and we dipped our back tires in the Pacific, that's another corny thing you do, because then you're supposed to dip your front tires in the Atlantic when you get there. Which I have not done yet, incidentally, don't know why. And I got a little video of him dipping his back tire and pretending to fall off this rock into the sea because he was a fucking clown, you know, he was a gifted physical comedian, he could have done that for real.

And then there are all the pictures of him I don't remember taking, and maybe losing those is worse than losing the ones I do.

(Silence.)

It took them about forty-five minutes to get him out, and the funny thing was he hadn't sustained any trauma to his head or anything but he had been face down in the mud with hundreds of pounds of weight on him and he had suffocated.

(Silence.)

So the part that everyone's pissed at me about is that after I filled out all the paperwork at the police station and called his mom and my mom I got back on my bike and kept riding.

(Long silence.)

VERA: I'm not wearing my hearing aid. So I could only hear parts of what you said. But I didn't want to interrupt.

(He lies down on the couch with his head in Vera's lap.)

Scene 8

Vera is on the phone, sitting with pen and paper in hand.

VERA: Are you sure that's it?
     I don't think that sounds right.
     I said I don't think that sounds right.

(A long pause, in which Vera becomes gradually more taken aback.)

Is that what I said? I didn't say I don't appreciate your looking it up for me, I do appreciate that. I just said I don't think that sounds right. And it's a cause I've been giving to for a long time, so I would think I would recognize the address.

(Brief pause.)

Well it doesn't! If it doesn't sound right, I'm not supposed to say so? Just to be polite?

(Brief pause.)

How should I know? Maybe you picked up the wrong piece of paper, or it's from an old, whaddayacallit.

(Brief pause.)

No, I don't know what it is, if I did I wouldn't have called you, now that's really a stupid question.

(She moves the phone away from her ear, and perhaps we can hear Ginny yelling, though we can't distinguish what she's saying.)

Oh for crying out loud, just tell it to me again, I'll say that's wonderful, that sounds exactly right, and I really owe you, Ginny, for taking two minutes out of your busy life to give me the wrong goddamn address. *(She is poised to write)*
Hello?
Ginny?

(Furious, Vera goes to the phone and hangs up. She thinks about it for a moment, then picks up and dials Ginny's number—it's a rotary phone, so it takes a long time. She waits. Maybe we can hear Ginny's phone ringing distantly across the hall, and her answering machine picking up. Vera speaks with utter, cool clarity.)

Hello, Ginny, I know you're there and you're not picking up because you're like a child. Anyway, I wanted to let you know that there's no need to call me from now on because with my grandson here I'm really very well taken care of and I don't need anyone else checking in. And since it's obviously so difficult for you to be in touch with me I think that's best.

155

(She hangs up. She is immediately remorseful. She brings her hand to her mouth. Leo enters. He touches her head on his way into the kitchen. Vera picks up the phone again, thinks, then hangs up. Leo reenters with orange juice.)

LEO: Ginny?

(She nods absently, and puts her hearing aid back in.)

Don't you ever just go over there and knock on the door? You know she's like twenty feet away.

VERA: For some reason we've never done that. Some idea she has about privacy, or . . .

(She trails off.)

LEO: You okay?

VERA: My files are such a mess. It's the time of the year I usually do all my donations and I can't find the list of charities I give to and I can't find my checkbook, so. That's the kind of morning I'm having.

LEO: I can help you look if you still haven't found it when I get back.

VERA: Where are you going?

LEO: Climbing wall, garden, interview.

VERA: Interview? For what?

LEO: For a job.

(Brief pause.)

VERA: Well I think that's pretty terrific. You're thinking about getting a part-time job, is that it?

LEO: Full-time. Very full-time.

VERA: I never thought I'd see the day!

LEO: Hey, I have no aversion to work, it's just gotta be the right job.

VERA: Where is it?

LEO: Rockies.

VERA: What?

LEO: Rocky Mountains.

VERA *(Hiding her disappointment)*: Oh.

LEO: They're looking for counselors, they have this program where they drop a bunch of rich kids in the mountains, they have to get from one point to another, rich kids have no idea what the fuck's what, they need leaders, so.

It's actually a pretty cool program, I did it in high school. Gotta say I think I'm very qualified, I think I have a good shot.

VERA: So when would that start?

LEO: Not till next summer.

VERA *(Relieved)*: Oh.

LEO: But I'd go out early, spend the winter on the slopes, there's always work for people like me.

VERA: So when would you leave?

LEO: I don't know. Soon.

VERA: I see.

(Pause.)

You know, you really haven't given the city a chance, you haven't done any of the museums, or the theater—

LEO: Grandma, come on.

VERA: I'm not trying to convince you of anything, I'm just making an observation. It's a great place to live and you haven't had the experience of it, not really.

LEO: I'm like a caged bird here, Vera, it's nothing against your city, but for me it's like a concrete prison.

VERA: Oh that's just a lot of—whaddayacallit—new-age baloney and you should listen to yourself once in a while because you sound stupid, you really do.

(*A silence. Leo exits into his bedroom. After a moment, he reenters with his backpack.*)

LEO: So I'll be back in a few hours, and then if you still need help looking for your, uh . . .

VERA: You didn't take it, did you?

LEO: What?

VERA: My checkbook.

Listen, I'll be a lot less angry if you tell me now.

LEO (*Smiling*): I didn't take it.

(*Pause.*)

VERA: Leo Joseph-Connell—

LEO: I didn't take it! I didn't take it I didn't take it I didn't take it. Yesterday you lost your keys, there were three days you couldn't find your hearing aid, there was the priceless morning your teeth went missing, you think I took those, too? I didn't take your fucking checkbook. God.

(*Pause.*)

VERA: I hope you're telling the truth, I really do. Your records of how much money you've taken haven't exactly been . . . I wasn't going to say anything, but . . .

(*Pause.*)

LEO: Well let's hope this interview goes well, because it's clear you don't trust me and it would be better for both of us if I got out of here.

VERA: Maybe that's true.

LEO: Maybe.

VERA: If you're going to the garden before the—you should bring a change of clothes because you always get filthy there.

leo: I thought of that.
vera: You did.
　　Well.

(She gazes off absently. He exits. The noise of the door closing startles her.)

Scene 9

Leo on Skype. It's late in the afternoon. He sits in front of an open laptop in a corner of the apartment.

LEO: Can you hear me? Lily? Can you—oh, hey. *(He waves once, slowly, smiling)* I can see that big smile but I can't hear you. Oh, hold up—

(He hits the volume key several times. We hear Lily's voice very faintly through the monitor.)

LILY *(Off)*: . . . can just call me—
LEO: Hey! There / it is—
LILY *(Off)*: Hey!
LEO: Hey, Sis, yeah.

(A pause. He smiles genuinely. Lily laughs through the monitor.)

LILY *(Off)*: Where's Grandma?

LEO: She's out shopping.

LILY *(Off)*: What kind of computer does she have?

LEO: It's a . . . *(He looks)* It's a MacBook, it's pretty new, actually. She still had that plastic covering on the screen.

(Laughter from Lily through the computer.)

She's so scared of it, she probably thought if she took it off the whole thing would fall apart. *(More laughter)* I've been trying to get her to use it so she'll have more . . . because I've been here three weeks now and I know there are some days if I wasn't here she wouldn't see anyone. What am I talking about how are you how are you how / are you.

LILY *(Off)*: I'm okay—

LEO: I'm sorry I haven't been in touch—

LILY *(Off)*: Yeah, Mom's really—

LEO: Can we not talk about Mom?

LILY *(Off)*: . . . okay.

(A silence. He lifts the computer and angles it around the room, allowing her to see the apartment.)

LEO: You remember this place?

LILY *(Off)*: . . . yeah.

(Brief pause.)

LEO: You remember singing at Grandpa's memorial service?

LILY *(Off)*: . . . vaguely.

LEO: Aunt Beth brought that shitty Casio and accompanied you, badly. *(Lily laughs)* You sang "The Water Is Wide." In English *and* in French.

LILY *(Off)*: I can't believe / you remember that.

LEO: I was proud of you. You brought some talented fucking genetic code with you into this family.

(A pause. Maybe we can hear Lily sigh.)

I was thinking you should maybe come out here for a while. Stay with Grandma. They gotta have like the / best voice teachers in the world here—

LILY *(Off)*: Wait, you're cutting out. / Leo, I can't hear you. Can you hear me?

LEO: Can you hear me? Lil, can you still not hear me? Yeah, I can hear you.

LILY *(Off)*: Oh there you are.

LEO: You can hear me again?

LILY *(Off)*: Now I can, yeah.

LEO: Sorry, I'm jacking a neighbor's wi-fi, I'm only getting like / one bar.

LILY *(Off)*: It's okay.

(Pause. He smiles at her, presumably getting a big, sad smile back.)

LEO: So I, hey, I wanted to ask, um, are you . . . ? In therapy? I mean it's cool, obviously it's cool if you are.

I just. I wondered if, uh, and this is probably really stupid? If, and obviously it's not just one thing, but if, like, it had to do with . . .

When I was home, earlier this summer, and we had that party, and we were fucked-up? . . .

LILY *(Off)*: Um . . . I . . . I don't know / if I . . .

LEO: No, yeah, I get that. I mean, I guess that's why you go to therapy, right, so you *don't* have to talk about these things with your immediate . . .

But if it was that—thing, (let me just say this,) I would like to apologize, and say I one hundred percent feel like a dick if that was weird or awkward or made you feel less like my *actual* sister, which obviously you are. Because I think you're like the greatest sister known to human history and

I would like to not have fucked at least that one thing up, okay? Lil?

LILY *(Off)*: . . . please come home . . .

LEO: Yeah, I just . . . I have to give some thought to whether that would be the best thing for everyone. And I don't just mean me, I mean Mom, and you, and . . . everyone.

But I'll think about it. It would be good to see you.

Yeah, I'm gonna hang up now, sorry.

(He closes the laptop. He takes a breath and regains control. The phone rings. Sure it is Lily calling back, he shakes it out, grins and picks up.)

Yeah, hey, sorry 'bout that. Hello? *(He listens)* Hello? Who is this? I'm sorry, I . . . I can't understand what you're saying.

(Pause. Discomfited, he hangs up. He gets the laptop and begins to head toward Vera's room to put it back. He is stopped by the sound of a sickening thud (and maybe something breaking) in the direction of Ginny's apartment. He stands still, listening. It's silent. He continues to Vera's room with the laptop. After a moment, he returns without the laptop. He sits on the couch, uneasy.

A long while passes. He listens, but there is no more sound. He makes a decision, stands and goes to Ginny's door. He knocks.)

Scene 10

Mid-afternoon, a few days later.

   Leo is wearing a suit that is too big and from an era long past—
Joe's.

   Vera enters from her bedroom, also dressed up.

VERA: Five minutes?
LEO: Whenever you're ready.
VERA: I just have to make peepee.

   *(She is about to exit, but sees something. She comes over to Leo
   to fix his tie. He lets her.)*

   I found my checkbook. You don't need to say anything,
   I was wrong about that, and I'm sorry.
LEO: I do owe you some money. I didn't write it down where
   you said but I know how much it is. I'll pay you back.
VERA: Maybe you will, maybe you won't. But I appreciate your
   saying so. *(She finishes his tie)*

I wish I could say you look just like him, but you really don't. You look more like your father's side of the family.

LEO: Sorry.

VERA: But you look good. *(She does a Brooklyn accent)* You clean up real nice!

LEO: I feel like a clown.

VERA: You look a little bit like a clown, but you look good.

(She is about to exit.)

LEO: Grandma.

VERA: Hm?

LEO: You can see your bra, through that shirt.

VERA: I know. This is the bra I wear with this shirt, because it goes.

(She exits into the bathroom. The buzzer sounds. He looks off, then decides to answer himself.)

LEO: Hello?

BEC *(Through the intercom)*: It's Bec.

(After a moment of uncertainty, he buzzes her in. He looks at himself, sorta freaks out, takes off his jacket, starts to unbutton his pants.)

LEO: Fuck it.

(He puts his jacket back on. He tousles his own hair. He tries to look casual. A knock at the door.)

It's open.

(Bec enters. She is wearing bike shorts and a long-sleeved jersey. She is carrying her bike helmet.)

BEC: Hey.

LEO: . . . hey.

BEC: Nice suit.

LEO: Thanks. Nice jersey.

BEC: Thanks.

(Pause.)

LEO: Uh . . .

BEC: So this is really stupid, I should've called, I thought you might want to go on a bike ride, but you're obviously busy.

LEO: Yeah. Yeah, I am kind of busy.

BEC: Okay, so. Sorry. Never mind.

(She goes to leave.)

LEO: Uh. I would say we could go tomorrow, but I'm heading out.

BEC: Where?

LEO: Back to St. Paul for a couple days, face up to the family. Then to Colorado.

BEC: What's in Colorado?

LEO: Got a job.

BEC: Congratulations.

LEO: Yeah, I think it's gonna be cool. Clarifying. Mountain air and all that.

BEC: That's great, I'm really happy for you.

LEO: Thanks. Yeah.

If you could wait maybe a couple hours—?

BEC: I have class.

LEO: Right. Class.

(Pause.)

BEC: It's just, I thought maybe you'd want to dip your front tire.

166

LEO: Ah.

BEC: Because you asked me to go with you that night you showed up at my dorm, and I was not in a frame of mind to . . . but you've probably already done it by now.

LEO: No, it's been kinda crazy around here, my grandma's needed me a lot. Her neighbor died. That's where we're—

BEC: I'm so sorry.

LEO: Not your fault.

BEC: I know.

Well. You probably won't have time, but, I printed a couple maps. Depending on where you want to do it. I know open ocean is ideal but around here I think you're gonna have to settle for bay.

LEO: I think as long as it's salty it counts.

BEC: I'm actually, one of the classes I'm taking, it's an anthropology class about ritual? Like in societies all over the world, and how it, on like a psychological and even neurological basis, it . . . well we're not that far into the class yet, but basically every culture has them and that's because they work. I don't know, I think if you can fit it in, you should do it.

(She hands him the maps.)

LEO: Thanks.

(The sound of a toilet flushing. Vera enters, putting pearls over her head. She sees Bec.)

VERA: Oh.

BEC: Hi.

VERA: Hello.

(Vera looks to Leo, who doesn't explain.)

LEO: You ready?

VERA: Just about.

LEO: I'm just gonna grab the notes for my speech.

(He exits. Vera is thoroughly mystified.)

VERA: You're coming, is that it?

BEC: No. I was just . . . no.
     I'm sorry about your neighbor.

VERA: You know Leo was the one who brought her to the hospital. He took care of everything, he stayed with her until they brought her into the, whaddayacallit. He was really . . . he was very much a man. Oh I'm sorry, you don't like it when I put it that way.

BEC: No, I'm actually glad to hear it.

VERA: He's leaving tomorrow, I guess he told you. Which does not make me very happy.

BEC: I'm sorry.

VERA: You'd think at my age I'd know better than to get used to anything. *(Off Bec's stricken look)* Oh don't look at me like that, I'll be all right, I've always been all right.

BEC: I know, I wasn't . . . *pitying* you, or—

VERA: Well you were, but never mind.

BEC: I wasn't, please don't think that.

VERA: All right, I always manage to upset you, let's forget I said anything.

BEC: You didn't upset me, I mean it's not you, I'm just irretrievably sad right now, and I know it's gonna pass, I know that, but it's very *convincing*, while it lasts, you know? It just feels very very real.

VERA: Well it is real. That's why. But you're right. It'll pass.

(Leo reenters, unaware of what he is interrupting.)

LEO: Okay!
     (Off their look) What?

(Pause.)

BEC: Bye, Leo.

(Brief pause.)

LEO: Bye.

(They hug deeply. Vera averts her eyes.)

BEC: Bye Vera.
VERA: Take care of yourself.

(Bec exits. A long pause.)

What's this about a speech?
LEO: I wasn't sure if they were gonna open it up to people in the audience. But just in case. You said she doesn't have a lot of people.
VERA: But did you ever meet her? I mean, before—?
LEO: No. You're right, it's probably not a good idea.
VERA: I think it's a lovely idea, I'm just surprised. Do you want to practice? We have a few minutes.
LEO: Uh . . . *(He looks at the paper)* Nah.
VERA: You should always practice before public speaking. Joe would've told you that.
LEO: Okay, um . . .
    I feel weird. Um.
    (Reading) Ginny was my grandmother's across / the hall—
VERA: Loudly, please.

(Brief pause.)

LEO: Ginny was my grandmother's across the hall neighbor, and they used to call each other every night to check in. Which I know gave my mom and my uncles a lot of solace, that there was someone my grandma talked to every day. But I don't want to make it sound like that was Ginny's only purpose in life, because actually a Google search revealed a varied and fascinating past. Ginny was an actress a long time ago, and she understudied for a play on Broadway called *Mary Had a Little. (To Vera)* You didn't tell me that.

(Vera nods.)

After that she started working for the William Morris Agency, as a secretary. So I guess she decided if she wasn't making it as an actor she wanted to help other actors make it, which I think is a pretty productive way of dealing with that kind of disappointment. Also she was married to a man who was killed in the Korean War. And after that I think she didn't get married again? . . .

(He looks to Vera, who nods.)

So I don't know, but I bet that was really terrible, and I know she was a peace activist, like my grandma, so I guess she came at that from a pretty personal angle. That's all I could find on the internet but she was eighty-one years old so there was a lot of other stuff, too.

(Pause.)

I guess that's not such a good ending.
VERA: It needs maybe one more . . . / whaddayacallit.
LEO: Yeah.

(They think, for kind of a long time.)

VERA: It's hard, because the truth is she was a pain in the ass.

(Pause.)

I guess you could say . . . you could say something about all her plants.

LEO: Oh yeah, I saw, in her apartment, there was like a / forest.

VERA: She would get a, whaddayacallit, that green slimy thing from California, with a stone / in it—

LEO: An avocado?

VERA: She would get an avocado at the supermarket, and put the stone in some water with those, uh, toothpicks, and next thing you know it's a tree.

What is that expression?

(She thinks.)

Green thumb.

(She is relieved to have thought of this.)

She was a pain in the ass, but God, she was like a magician. That woman could make anything grow.

(Leo listens, and then writes. Lights fade.)

END OF PLAY

AMY HERZOG's plays include *After the Revolution* (Williamstown Theatre Festival; Playwrights Horizons; Lilly Award), *4000 Miles* (Lincoln Center; Obie Award for the Best New American Play), *The Great God Pan* (Playwrights Horizons) and *Belleville* (Yale Repertory Theatre; New York Theatre Workshop; finalist for the Susan Smith Blackburn Prize). She has received commissions from Yale Repertory Theatre, Steppenwolf Theatre Company and Playwrights Horizons. Amy is a recipient of the Whiting Writers' Award, the Benjamin H. Danks Award from the American Academy of Arts and Letters, the Helen Merrill Award, the Joan and Joseph F. Cullman Award for Extraordinary Creativity and the *New York Times* Outstanding Playwright Award. She is a Usual Suspect at New York Theatre Workshop and an alumna of Youngblood at Ensemble Studio Theatre, Play Group at Ars Nova and the SoHo Rep Writer/Director Lab. She has taught playwriting at Bryn Mawr and Yale, and received an MFA from the Yale School of Drama.